D0039876

PENETRATING
the
DARKNESS

PENETRATING *the* DARKNESS

*Discovering the Power of the Cross
Against Unseen Evil*

Jack Hayford
with
Rebecca Hayford Bauer

Chosen

a division of Baker Publishing Group
Grand Rapids, Michigan

Penetrating the Darkness
Copyright © 2011
Jack W. Hayford

Cover design: Kirk DouPonce, DogEaredDesign.com
Cover imagery: DigitalVision

Unless otherwise identified, Scripture quotations are from the New King James Version. Copyright © 1982 by Thomas Nelson, Inc. Used by permission. All rights reserved.

Scripture quotations identified THE MESSAGE are from *The Message*. Copyright © by Eugene H. Peterson 1993, 1994, 1995, 1996, 2000, 2001, 2002. Used by permission of NavPress Publishing Group.

Scripture quotations in the foreword are from THE HOLY BIBLE, NEW INTERNATIONAL VERSION,® NIV® Copyright © 1973, 1978, 1984, 2010 by Biblica, Inc.™ Used by permission. All rights reserved worldwide.

Scripture quotations identified KJV are from the King James Version of the Bible.

All rights reserved. No part of this publication may be reproduced, stored in a retrieval system or transmitted in any form or by any means—electronic, mechanical, photocopying, recording or otherwise—without the prior written permission of the publisher. The only exception is brief quotations in printed reviews.

Published by Chosen Books
11400 Hampshire Avenue South
Bloomington, MN 55438
www.chosenbooks.com

Chosen Books is a division of
Baker Publishing Group, Grand Rapids, Michigan.

Printed in the United States of America

Library of Congress Cataloging-in-Publication Data

Hayford, Jack W.
    Penetrating the darkness : discovering the power of the cross against unseen evil / Jack Hayford with Rebecca Hayford Bauer.
      p. cm.
    ISBN 978-0-8007-9453-8 (pbk. : alk. paper) 1. Spiritual warfare. 2. Jesus Christ—Crucifixion. I. Bauer, Rebecca Hayford. II. Title.
    BV4509.5.H39   2011
    235'.4—dc22

2010048208

In keeping with biblical principles of creation stewardship, Baker Publishing Group advocates the responsible use of our natural resources. As a member of the Green Press Initiative, our company uses recycled paper when possible. The text paper of this book is comprised of 30% post-consumer waste.

green
press
INITIATIVE

DEDICATION AND
ACKNOWLEDGMENT

To great prayer warriors in the spiritual battle against evil's darkness. The God-given victories of these listed impacted multitudes for Christ and altered the course of local and regional history where they ministered; they shaped my own prayer life and role as a pastor—both in public and in private. Each held a unique place in my life experience and in dedicating this book to them—most of whom have gone on to their heavenly reward—I bow in praise to God for their lives and their faithfulness to "prayer and to the ministry of the Word" (Acts 6:4).

- First, to my mother, Dolores Hayford—who taught me to obey God's Word, walk with Jesus every day and listen to the Holy Spirit always.

- To pastors—Earl Sexauer, of my pre-college years; Kenneth Erickson, during my first years as a church planter; then Dr. Roy Hicks Sr. and Dr. Herman Mitzner—who, with those pastors, each had large input to my life through their own unique teaching, model, manner.

- To missionaries—most notably to Dr. Jean Darnall, Drs. Jean and John Firth and Dr. Evelyn Thompson, who all being warm and gracious people, but also strong contenders "for the faith once for all delivered to the saints" (Jude 3): They each changed nations through prayer!

- To members of the wonderful pastoral team and elders at The Church On The Way, as well as devoted members such as Jim and Carol Owens, whom God used to spread what the Holy Spirit was teaching that congregation throughout the 1970s. God welded a pursuit of intercessory prayer (with amazing, confirming results) that was established then and continues faithfully and effectively to this day.

- Primarily, to my dear "Lady Anna": my near-lifelong prayer partner. She has been at my side in prayer for 56 years, faithfully and patiently bearing the prayer needs that daily appear on the agenda of any pastor—needs that are all the more numerous when that pastorate becomes numbered in the thousands.

- Finally—it is a profound joy to see all of our four children and eleven grandchildren walking with Christ and raising their children in His way. They are "good kids" whom Jesus has kept, and who reveal the joyous outcome of daily prayer and pivotal times of parental intercession unto spiritual breakthrough.

It is also fitting that our "firstborn," and thereby first to begin learning and living the truths and principles herein, has contributed so greatly to the writing of this book—my daughter Rebecca Hayford Bauer. Her editorial aid was infinitely more than technical, but introduced insightful content because she has "lived out" these concepts herself, practically, parentally and in pastoral work. Without her help, neither the scope nor the timeliness of this work would be complete.

I thank the Father for each of these. Their lives touched mine and have added a touch that will hopefully enrich you as they each did me.

JACK W. HAYFORD, AT THANKSGIVING, 2010

CONTENTS

FOREWORD

Wow! The rules of engagement have been captured from the U.S. Armed Forces by Jack Hayford; but unlike the U.S. Marines, he takes no prisoners!

The devil and all his cohorts are identified and dealt with—military style! From "Back to Basics," "Boot Camp" and "Intercession" to "The Blood of Jesus," "A Binding Contract," "Breaking Loose" and actually "Engaging in Battle," Pastor Jack shows us the way to *Penetrating the Darkness*.

And what a timely word this is. Clearly, our enemy has "come down with great fury" (Revelation 12:12). *"Why now?"* you ask? He knows "his time is short" (Revelation 12:12). "Invasion of Life"—your life is his goal! Surely the evening newscast shows us clearly that the darkness grows darker! But the final chapter raises us up with Jesus as Commander-in-Chief. Praise God: "WE SHALL DO VALIANTLY" (last chapter)!

If you expect to win your battles, and I know you have them, Jack Hayford's new book is some anointed new ordnance (ammunition) to win the battle every time!

Read on and let's all give the devil TROUBLE!

Paul F. Crouch, President
Trinity Broadcasting Network

1

RULES OF ENGAGEMENT

And take the helmet of salvation, and the sword of the Spirit,
which is the word of God; praying always with all prayer
and supplication in the Spirit.

EPHESIANS 6:17–18

Nothing has more greatly shaped the experiences and events of my life than prayer: *personal* prayer, *public* prayer gatherings, *pointed* and focused prayer, *passionate* prayer and *power-filled*, Spirit-energized prayer!

This kind of praying rises from more than simple devotion; it is born of a growing discipleship—availability to God's Word where understanding is gained through learning, joined to an acquired and expanding experience in applying its truth to real-life pursuit and practice of prayer. That is the kind Jesus taught. It is prayer that lifts praying well beyond the habits of multitudes who, when they do pray, are exercising more of something akin to rubbing a rabbit's foot. Then, others express a hope heavenward that "something good will happen" or that "this awful thing will go away"—a hope-against-hope, desperate call to a God irregularly consulted but now desperately needed.

Further, though we build the important basics of the believer's devotional prayer life, these pages extend the Savior's call to His people—to receive and employ "the keys of the Kingdom"; to enter an extended dimension of faith-grounded prayer. This introductory chapter is not only to invite you to a broadened perspective and an increased constancy in faith and the Word of God, but to set a framework of thought—or "the rules of engagement"— that I think may help. *Rules of engagement* is a military term that defines for commanders and troops when, where and how force will be used. I have chosen this term to title this chapter, not only because we are setting a framework into place, but also to send a clarion call that when we pray, we are, indeed, engaged in spiritual warfare.

SIMPLY PUT: IT'S A WAR

This order of prayer involves a biblical understanding of the continuing spiritual "struggle between kingdoms" and the spiritual discernment the Holy Spirit enables. In short, it is that kind of prayer the apostle Paul described as "praying with the understanding and with the Spirit." This will be helpful for engaging the invisible warfare between God's will for mankind and the evil design of the dark world of Satan's ploys.

The clash of good and evil, of God and Satan, or the Kingdom of God and powers of darkness is *there*—there in the Word of God. It is a battle over which some believers have puzzled themselves, saying, "Didn't Jesus 'win it all' at the cross? He said, 'It is finished.' " Bewildered by that, some have suggested that any mention of spiritual warfare trivializes the cross of Christ, but in fact, that is not the case.

- The epistles laud the cross and the blood of Christ as having completed salvation's provision, but they also teach that a spiritual conflict is being engaged in "this present evil age" (Galatians 1:4).

- The blood of the cross is not only honored, but its power is testified to as the source of authority that equips believers to prevail in this present age-long battle against "that serpent of old, called the Devil and Satan, who deceives the whole world" (Revelation 12:9).

- All prayer—petition, intercession, supplication and praiseful thanksgiving—is noted as "the weapons of our warfare," as believers gird for the battle in spiritual armor and take up spiritual weaponry (see 2 Corinthians 10:3–5; Ephesians 6:10–18).

ENLISTING "KINGDOM WARRIORS"

Central to understanding the resources and tactical weapons the Word of God describes as essential in this conflict is the dual reminder within Jesus' words when on trial before Pilate. Being asked "Are you a king?" He affirmed He is, but He qualified His kingship as being over a spiritual Kingdom—the Kingdom of God. We will take time to study the reality of this invisible Kingdom, the history of the warfare being waged and the strategies employed by each side.

The Lord of the Church is the King of a kingdom—the Kingdom of God. The message and ministry of that Kingdom was at the heart of everything Jesus did—His preaching, teaching, healing, casting out of demons, forgiving, freeing and initiating the founding of His Church. He was explicit that what He began in the ministry and penetration of His Kingdom of love, life, truth and grace was to continue beyond His death, resurrection and ascension through His people. That "people" includes you and me, along with all the redeemed, discipled, Spirit-empowered and commissioned Body—the "troops" within His Church. He said:

> And this gospel of the kingdom will be preached in all the world as a witness to all the nations, and then the end will come.
>
> MATTHEW 24:14

> Most assuredly, I say to you, he who believes in Me, the works that I do he will do also; and greater works than these he will do, because I go to My Father. And whatever you ask in My name, that I will do, that the Father may be glorified in the Son. If you ask anything in My name, I will do it.
>
> JOHN 14:12–14

These basic texts join to Jesus' announcement of His plan to "build My Church" (see Matthew 16:13–18). It is in that context that our Lord also relates His basic strategy for the Church's advance unto spiritual victory as the powers of hell are rendered unable to prevail.

As we traverse the Scriptures together, we will draw alongside Jesus' own disciples as He taught them about the Kingdom, and will discover how essential it is that we perceive how *real* the invisible war is, and how *adequate* the resources He provides for us through prayer—unto "penetrating the darkness."

IT IS DARKER THAN EVER

In a very real sense, the words of the title of this book could appropriately be used to provide a subtitle for the Bible. All of the Word of God is a story—from the Creation to the Consummation, from the chaotic darkness "upon the face of the deep" to the glories of the eternal city where *forever* "the Lamb is the Light thereof."

Today, the Bible's prophecies of the end times declare the challenge between, on the one hand, the increasing enterprises of evil and dark powers that corrupt humanity, and the inky blackness of hell's demons surfacing for the final conflict (see 1 Timothy 4:2; 2 Timothy 3:1–5, 13; Revelation 9:1–21). On the other hand are those who answer Christ's call as the Lord of the Church for us to overcome (see 1 John 5:4–5)!

The darkness is deepening—but the Word of God sounds a trumpet blast of faith-inspiring promise: *Where sin abounds, grace much more abounds!* It is the grace that flows from the cross and the grace that flowed to each of us who have met the Savior there. And it is also the same grace, filling and overflowing each of us who open to those overflowing "streams of living water," that is available to every believer who will receive that full endowment of the Holy Spirit Jesus prophesied. It is the "river" that provides power to live for Christ, to grow in the Word and prayer, and power to follow the Kingdom's King—Jesus—as He leads us to "stand, therefore," becoming equipped for battle.

In His name, by the Word of His promise and by the blood of His cross through which He triumphed over the authority of all dark powers, let us learn and apply His triumph. Those are the grounds, and His power in the Spirit is the way. Applied in prayer in simple faith made bold through the truth it can—and will—pierce like a sword, cut through the bonds of darkness and release the lost from shame, futility, enslaving addiction, sickness and eternal loss.

2

THE GIFT OF A KINGDOM

I bestow upon you a kingdom,
just as My Father bestowed one upon Me.

LUKE 22:29

The message of "the Kingdom of God" is the constant theme of the message Jesus preached and the lessons He taught.

He came proclaiming the *power* and *presence* of the Kingdom as the "entry" of God's *will* and *rule,* here to impact *every* situation. He applied Kingdom grace and power regarding every need or circumstance: health and healing, sin and forgiveness, human relationships, personal character, human failure, divine provision and His call for us to grow in faith. His message at every point was to give hope. He came to bring "life abundantly"—life at a new dimension—both present and future. And He offered the gift of a Kingdom to all who would accept it—a dual offer of *salvation,* to birth us into the Kingdom, and the gift of *partnership,* to enable us as "citizens" to extend His Kingdom into all the world. So when He stood on the shores of Galilee, or taught on the Temple grounds in Jerusalem, He proclaimed His message with a sin-shattering, life-transforming possibility.

Consider the implications of these three key phrases in which Jesus speaks, calling us—now and then—to hear, understand and act *what* "the Kingdom of God" is about, and *how* He wants us as His disciples to learn to draw on Kingdom power and apply its gracious works through prayer.

- *"The kingdom of God has come upon you"* (Luke 11:20). Jesus is saying that because He—the King—was/is present, His Kingdom's potential to *penetrate* whatever need exists with His personal grace, forgiveness, healing or peace is also present—that is, if and wherever hearing hearts welcome Him into their lives or situations. In short, He's saying, "*My* world (Kingdom) is ready to change *your* world if you are willing and will ask."

- *"Unless one is born of water and the Spirit, he cannot enter the kingdom of God"* (John 3:5). Jesus' answer to Nicodemus' sincere question, despite the man's religious training and experience, introduces His call to new birth. He makes very clear that with His arrival as *Messiah* (i.e., God's anointed King-Savior-Deliverer), participation in the Kingdom requires "birth" into it. His message always confronted our most basic human need—forgiveness of sin, repentance and faith. Now we are invited to *receive* the Gospel of the Kingdom and thereby *accept* Him—receiving and welcoming the King's presence and rule in our lives.

- *"The kingdom of heaven is at hand"* (Matthew 4:17). The *presence* of the King is the point. Any place He's welcome, He will *enter* and work "the Father's will"—on earth (where you are) as it is in heaven, which is nearer "at hand" because God is not distant. Its blessing and transforming power, character and qualities are within the circle of the hearer's reach or access.

Our privilege of *access* is explained when Jesus begins to teach about His Church, about how He will *build* it and how He intends us, the same as His early disciples, to confront the workings of evil. He specifically expressed His will to give "access" to each of us who come to Him, saying, *"I will build My church, and the gates of Hades shall not prevail against it. And I will give you the keys of the kingdom of heaven"* (Matthew 16:18–19).

This is the basic text at the heart of the idea of "spiritual warfare" and is foundational to our understanding of what He has called us to do in penetrating the darkness of our world. The Bible often refers to the struggle of life against death, God's right way (righteousness) against evil (sin and Satan's destructive ways), in terms of warfare, of spiritual conflict—of Light against the Darkness. So here, where Jesus first announces the place He calls each of us to participate (to "partner"), we need to grasp the depth of importance in His words yet embrace the practical simplicity with which He describes our role as one of His own—as citizens born into His Kingdom.

The word-picture Jesus uses of *keys* signifies His release to His Church of both access and authority. If you have keys—and most of us have a pocketful!—it indicates areas of your life where access has been granted to you. Most likely you have keys to an office, your home and your car. There may be files that you keep locked, or a mailbox. The fact that you *have* those keys reveals the fact that you have the authority, or the right, to access those particular places or possessions.

For example, the majority of us own a car, and yet we know that we cannot drive that car unless we utilize keys. The vehicle can sit in the garage unused, though inherent in its availability to you is your capacity to utilize all that the car was designed to do. The car's potential or power, however, will only be activated when you use the keys: Access allows for advance, but progress requires participation.

It is admittedly a humbling proposition for the Son of God to say, "You are not only given the keys, but your choice to use them is *the* 'key' to the active release of My Kingdom's advance 'on earth as it is in heaven.'" So as we move into this book, I want to frame and underscore a mindset toward *humility,* but one that does not diminish our consciousness of the awesome authority we've been called to apply—in prayer and in daily life and service for Jesus. Let me illustrate.

When my children were teenagers, they were given access to the use of the family car. They each had done nothing to provide that vehicle for the family or to keep it in operating order. The use of the car was made available as they grew in understanding and responsibility, and the privilege was given to them. Their "authority" was not "usurped" or taken by selfish assertion. It was granted because they were obedient sons and daughters. In other words, though they had not provided anything to acquire it, keys were given to them, and full use granted by the will of their father.

However, with that privilege came a need for the balance of *wisdom* in how they drove and the need to avoid "thinking they're smart" because they had use of the car. That right didn't mean they could loan it to anyone else or get into a street race. Their privilege was not intended to raise kids who pompously paraded their "authority to use the keys" or what they were or were not allowed to do. The keys are for the use of the family's interests and benefit, as well as for those with or around us.

When Jesus said that He was giving the keys of the Kingdom of heaven to His Church, He was offering His children access to the power of God's Kingdom and authority over the darkness of evil. The "car keys" picture is helpful to keep us impressed with the *privilege* of the keys and the *practice* of their use; not with *our* power but with our Lord's. Yet though we have done nothing to earn or acquire this privilege of being given the "keys of the Kingdom," our Lord has provided them and called us to use them, releasing authority to us through the blood of His cross and in His name.

Everything about the Kingdom has been opened to us through the cross. We can receive nothing without first opening to salvation, new birth, forgiveness and freedom from sin. But just as physical birth issues forth into growth, life and possibility, so does new birth. It is that birth by the renewing and regenerating power of the Holy Spirit that brings about the possibility of our seeing—understanding—and entering the Kingdom, becoming an active participant in advancing the rule of God's will. That rule brings a flow of life, grace, forgiveness and power that will always unfold God's loving will for humankind, and will overthrow the evil workings of the flesh and the devil that were unleashed upon earth at "the Fall"—or the downfall of humankind as a result of Adam's sin. [Dear Reader: If you have any question about whether you have been *truly* "born" into the Kingdom of God, let me urge you to turn to the brief pages at the very end of this book, to see how you can "enter" and live with confidence into a "now and forever" relationship with Him.]

GAINING THE LARGER PICTURE

Our pursuit of prayer that penetrates the darkness, and applies the power of the cross in Jesus' name with Holy Spirit-empowered prayer, will be aided by gaining a grasp of a well-grounded perspective on the biblical concept of the Kingdom of God.

Having taken an introductory snapshot of the Kingdom already, let's go further to see what was being introduced by our

Lord Jesus as He began "teaching [and] preaching the gospel of the kingdom" (Matthew 4:23). It will enable us to gain a larger picture of the full panorama of humankind—first of what had been planned and became aborted.

It is important to begin here, because much of the passivity or weakness of convictions about prayer is the result of either blindness or ignorance of basic truths concerning the Kingdom of God; of *how it was designed* for humankind's fulfillment through partnering with God's will for earth, and *how it became consigned* to ruin by "the flesh and the devil."

Through my decades of pastoral ministry and teaching, I have found that when this broadened picture is seen and grasped it changes the way people think and how they pray. Let's look at:

1. What the Father *intended* in the beginning
2. What was *upended*—overturned by sin's rebellion
3. What was *extended* through God's sending His Son to us
4. What was *expended* by Jesus' blood and death to redeem and recover it all

It helps establish deeper convictions about the power and privilege of prayer, and begins to shape a Kingdom mindset rooted in Kingdom truth. It cultivates "a Kingdom kind" of people or person, "believers" who are more than simply "nice people who have been born again and are going to go to heaven someday." All those blessings entail is wonderful, but along with finding peace with God and the promise of eternity with Him, we need—and Christ desires us—to discover that He has much, much more for us as the Father's children.

As His redeemed, we are called beyond "being saved" to enter the school of discipleship with Jesus, first by opening to an empowering encounter with the Holy Spirit. That baptism with the Spirit includes the availability of divine power to assist us in our living, our growth, our praying, our worship, our labors, our—well, you name it! The Holy Spirit has come to glorify Christ—to cause the fullness of Jesus' person and purpose to increase and graciously impact others around and beyond us where we live and for all that we pray (see Ephesians 3:16–19).

Further, when Kingdom truth about Kingdom rule is understood, not only does the beauty and wonder of Jesus' call to our partnership become dynamic: The clarity of a sound understanding about our source of power and privilege in His name will not become muddled or muddied by pride, arrogance or any confusion about our authority as granted by God within His ultimate and unlimited sovereignty. We will find security as well as emboldened authority in Christ as the grandeur of God's almightiness—His love, holiness, wisdom, power and grace is seen as ours in which to partner and to partake.

So come with me, and let us, as redeemed sons and daughters, come with humility to learn His works and ways that now invite us to rule with Him through Christ and His cross.

A stunning proposition, wouldn't you say?

You may, you know. This is what He meant for you when He invited you to a new life *now* in His Kingdom: *living on earth*—empowered to come before His throne, and *"in heaven"*—approaching with that bold humility and endowed authority with which He has willed we pray, to "release" His ruling power in answer to our prayer. It's *His* way to advance *His* will being done on earth—*where* we ask for it and *when* He is asked! So, to see how this partnership was His plan and will from the beginning, let's return there.

Just as you cannot chart a course forward if you do not know where you have been, our perspective on God's *original plan* for humankind will determine our perspective on His *present plan* through Jesus' coming as a human to earth, His purpose in the cross and His through His Church today. Let us examine something of the fuller dimensions to which Jesus wants to restore us in that plan now as He did in His ministry; otherwise, we will too easily settle for less than Jesus' purpose for and *through* each of us in His Body—His Church.

KINGDOM LOST

At Creation, God gave specific direction to the first human couple: "Be fruitful and multiply . . . have dominion" (Genesis 1:28). Humankind was called to spread the rule of God's Kingdom throughout the earth. Their home and their purpose were both defined for them. They lived in a Garden of perfection, specific parameters and fellowship with the living God. This was home. The work they were called to was to extend the rule of what was in the Garden to all of the planet. Their fellowship was with God; their loyalty was to Him; they were His hand on earth spreading His dominion.

As with any good parent, however, God did not want robotic obedience without the privileged responsibility of choice. So He bestowed on His human creation the gift of free will, and for free will to be effected, there had to be an option. Without rules there is no such thing as choice. But with obedience to God's will and ways, God's blessed, benevolent, beauty-filled purposes offered the highest and best for His creatures and creation.

Of course, we know now how Adam and Eve, like naive yet injury-prone children, opted to push the big red button that said *Don't push!* Pursuing their own way and will, and being blindly deceived by the serpent-liar, they yielded to self-will and plunged our entire planet off course. Their disobedience had staggering ramifications, not only cutting them off from their life-source of

God's enabling power, but short-circuiting His purposes for their fulfillment and for earth's best future.

KINGDOM RUINED

Everything about our planet became broken. Relationship between God and people was severed. Man's spirit died. The relationship between the man and the woman became one of blame and disunity. Rather than extending dominion throughout the earth, people were now reduced to trying to scratch a living out of the dirt. The quest to have more resulted in the abdication of Paradise.

In that moment, the world was immersed in confusion and exposure to the hateful and destructive ploys of the Adversary. Man was intended to rule the planet but now had forfeited humankind's rule to Satan the Adversary. God's intended purposes for earth were breached simultaneously with the broken relationship between God and man. The spiritual cataclysm resulting from the Fall of man through disobedience defies description. The cycle of pain, ruin, confusion, disease and death that overtook earth and humankind with Adam and Eve's sin and loss of relationship with God had an indescribably horrible threefold outcome:

- Humankind's loss of relationship and rulership, and the right to administer earth's affairs was betrayed to Satan!
- A released and ongoing spread of deception, of ruin and of all the things the kingdom of darkness can introduce was set in motion.
- A spiritual blindness beset our entire race, and, blinded by selfish interest, deluded by pride and supposed wisdom devoid of divine revelation, souls ignorantly submit to the liar.

The passage of time and the philosophies of man have occasioned either forgetfulness or disdain for God's Word and His revelation of the source of earth's and humankind's dilemma. As a result, either ignorance, pride or unbelief discards the insight that would lead to understanding and recovery, and multitudes fault God, "If there really is one . . . because if He exists, why does He permit such darkness to continue?" The bottom line is that He doesn't. The hellishness in our world is all a result of the decision made by Adam and ratified by all humankind—each by our own self-will. The administrative rights—intended, under God, to be benevolently blessed and faithfully administrated through man's fidelity to His will—were handed over to the Adversary, the devil, and continue to be exercised by a being who hates all that is God or is intended by Him.

All hellishness in our world is the result of his rule, not God's; but neither is God inactive. He is moving in the way He is because if He were simply to quash the rebellion in one mighty act, all of humankind would be destroyed and there would be none redeemed. The Scripture tells us, however, that God took action—choosing to recover the loss in a manner that would be a "win" for all who open to His kindness; that love and grace of God that, if received, will bring us to repentance—to a new life, a new hope, a new perspective on our world, a new desire to reach the needy in it, to show compassion and to bring them into salvation (see Romans 2:4). "The Lord is . . . not willing that any should perish but that all should come to repentance" (2 Peter 3:9).

The Redeemer appeared. Jesus, as Son of man, has come— the second Adam, God-with-us, the incarnate sinless Savior. He is here to continue His works of deliverance, forgiveness and power; here to unmask the Adversary and unchain his prisoners. Jesus announced, "The thief does not come except to steal, and to kill, and to destroy. . . . [But I have] come to seek and to save that which was lost" (John 10:10; Luke 19:10). He is the one who has led the charge to penetrate the darkness.

Thus the story changed. Instead of a permanent loss of God's rule on the planet mankind had been given, God set into action His plan of redemption—the plan to ultimately bring all of creation, all of us, back to His original purpose and plan.

KINGDOM COME

Ultimately the King will come and establish His rulership once and for all at His coming—the return of Christ. But in the meantime, He has appointed the ministry of all He has, is and wants to fulfill of the Father's will to His Church . . . to you and me. His parable of the householder who left for a time and promised to return, charging servants to "do business till I come," is also the charge before us. That "business" in prayer in Jesus' name can flow with a penetrating power that will only be released through "prayer that breaks through," that drives back the darkness, the demonic, the disease and deathly syndromes that proliferate everywhere. He calls us to be those who move in that dimension of spiritual life and authority. It is not enough for us to pray for Jesus to come back, though that is a spiritual directive as well: "The Spirit and the bride say, 'Come!'" (Revelation 22:17). Rather, *while* we await His return, our assignment is the business of prayer.

In Luke 19:11–13, Jesus describes the nobleman giving each of his servants the equivalent of nearly three years' salary in advance, to invest and multiply, until he returned. Today, the investment God has given you and me is that by His Spirit He "vests" us (clothes us) not only with garments of righteousness through forgiveness, but also with a wealth of "currency"—that is, an account to draw on of heaven's power through our prayer. It is to minister with Christ's authority, as well as His gentle spirit, to break through the strongholds of satanic darkness, whether it is entrenched in a soul of a person or steeped in the soul of a nation.

There are prayer strategies that can penetrate any type of situation. Not every obstacle is overcome at once, but we are called to a war, not a skirmish, and whether it fits your presuppositions or not, Christ Jesus has said to us, "Whatever you ask in My name, that I will do" (John 14:13).

KINGDOM NOW?

An ever-present danger arises with frequency whenever the subjects of "faith for Kingdom breakthrough" or "spiritual warfare" or "the believer's authority in prayer" are discussed. The problem centers on two questions. The first question rises from the realism that "Just because you pray or command an answer now, doesn't mean it is yours to dictate the timing." The second raises the question, "Isn't God sovereign—and isn't all power His, or aren't all outcomes under His control, or haven't they even been predetermined by reason of His mightiness? *Who are we to claim 'authority' and on what terms can anyone claim a place of 'ruling' in life's issues in this present world?*"

First, to allay any suspicious inquirers wondering if we are proposing a "Kingdom now" theology, that insinuates that a band of believers or the Church at large may "bring the Kingdom" on its own schedule or by its own advisement, forget it! We hold no such position nor teach any such doctrine.

However, the letter to the Romans is quite clear that the reign of our Savior, who died and rose again to break the bondage that deprives humankind of *both* a relationship with God *and* a ruling role or reign with Him, is a reign to which He invites us. It is available because what the first Adam lost, Christ—the second

Adam and founder of a new order within God's grace—has come to reclaim. Now He invites us to begin to learn and live in that rule during this lifetime.

> For if by the one man's offense death reigned through the one, much more those who receive abundance of grace and of the gift of righteousness will reign in life through the One, Jesus Christ . . . so that as sin reigned in death, even so grace might reign through righteousness to eternal life through Jesus Christ our Lord.
>
> ROMANS 5:17, 21

The tense of *reign* in Romans 5:21 indicates that there is a conditional nature of the prophetic pronouncement; that within the present, on the grounds of what Jesus Christ's sacrifice and obedience neutralized of the limits sin placed on human circumstances, actions may (or they might not) be taken on the grounds of Christ's victory as Lord of Life and King of Glory.

It is into that victory He invites us to reign in life, not as supposing we are "controllers of destiny," but as servants endowed with the authority to exercise administrative authority in situations put within the realm of our involvement or assignment. Where such is the case, believers have been given grounds to invoke the will of God's rule as "joint heirs with Christ" (Romans 8:17), which grants us full privileges to invoke *what He would do*—now. The presence of the Savior with us includes the present privilege of the promises of God to bring an entry of His Kingdom power into situations or circumstances for which we pray and in which we are ministering.

"Fear not, little flock; for it is your Father's good pleasure to give you the kingdom," Jesus said (Luke 12:32, KJV). The imagery of a *lamb* speaks volumes, just as His description of a little flock refuses to couch Kingdom in anything suggesting the power-systems of earth ways, works or wisdom. "The Kingdom" offers open access to reign as well as to live *now*, a prospect open to those who live in the spirit of the Lamb—*submitted* to the Father, *yielded* to His will, *gentle* in spirit and *guileless* as a lamb. To these our Lord and Master says, "Don't fear: Take the Kingdom keys and use them!"

To most effectively rise as one who may learn to penetrate the darkness in prayer or ministry, let "Christ in you" infuse you with the Holy Spirit of one who, being born into the bloodline of the Lamb of God, chooses to learn and live as one of His flock. It is these who are invited to "reign in life" now.

This is what we were "born again" to receive, to inherit and to live in. It is exciting and laden with blessings and joy. But it also needs more than foundational understanding.

It requires a life that is based in "the basics" of prayer, the Word and a growing faith.

3

BACK TO BASICS

For the eyes of the LORD are on the righteous,
and His ears are open to their prayers.

1 PETER 3:12

There was a season of my life when my prayer life had been so impacted by deepening dimensions of worship and intercession, that the *basic* practice of daily devotional prayer had been altered to the point that the Lord confronted me. It happened one morning as I had just turned off the alarm to rise for the very purpose of prayer. But I was about to receive a stark reminder. As I sat on the edge of the bed, the Lord spoke to me—simply, pointedly, uncondemningly: *You have forgotten the habit of daily devotional prayer.*

Notwithstanding the fact I was up for that very purpose— prayer—I understood precisely what He was saying: I was interceding, but I was not giving myself to the daily intimacy of time with Jesus. He was calling me to the basics of the believer's prayer life: the issues of life, ongoing duties and responsibilities, the "prayer list" of people and family, the "housekeeping of my heart," and my ongoing attention to the day-to-day realities of living.

In addressing the basics, then, I want to address the foundation points of a prayer life—however mundane or familiar they may seem to you. I want to ask you to walk with me through either a review of, or introduction to, the basics because they are the foundation from which any practice of refreshing worship should flow, and upon which a life that includes spiritual warfare should be built.

Perhaps you are as I was that morning—neglectful of the basics. But this can happen in any part of life. The basics of procedures at work. Or basic communication skills with those around us. We forget to exercise; and our bodies are the worse for it. Forgetting or overlooking the basics is a common malady of us all. In this case, I needed reminding . . . not "to pray," but to renew the devotional habit that was so basic it had been part of my understanding since youth and college years.

I learned to pray in childhood and have always pursued a believer's walk as a man who prays. I consult the Lord regularly, it not being uncommon for me to stop midstride of a task or call and put it before the Lord for His wisdom. I seek to be sensitive to respond to Holy Spirit promptings to intercession—to keep tuned for those times that He signals my soul to stop what I am doing and, even if but briefly, call on the Lord—praying for that issue.

So, in other words, it was not as though I did not pray at all. But the attention to given basics had faded somehow, even though my worship life and role as a spiritual warrior had become more vigilant and dynamic. I had not realized this, of course, and perhaps it was because I was mindful in new and broadened ways—seeking the Lord, yet captivated as it were by new dimensions of prayer.

The Lord taught me how vital the basics are to build *all* of life on as a person of prayer. So, in developing the truth of Kingdom authority, spiritual warfare and penetrating the darkness through applying the triumph of the cross, I want *first* to be certain that you know and wisely sustain the foundation of prayer—a daily walk with Jesus. This word picture says it all: The basics we are talking about, just like the footings of a foundation, make the difference metaphorically between being content to stand on a stone in the middle of a refreshing brook and enjoy the water flowing around us (as in worship's celebration and exaltation), and stepping out onto the solid rock of a Hoover Dam and being grounded at the center where the distribution of light-surged power and life-giving water is available to be directed as needed. In short, the breakthrough power of spiritual warfare, when it is directed by the Holy Spirit, most naturally and effectively flows when in between we are living a solid, day-to-day walk with Jesus—in life and in prayer.

THE FOUNDATION OF PRAYER

This foundational issue of a daily devotional time is found in the heartbeat of Jesus' life and ministry. He taught His disciples that the power of Kingdom life flows through prayer. His followers who experienced Pentecost and those who were part of the early Church's explosive growth were daily at prayer (see Acts 2:46). The life of power in His disciples today is likewise constantly nourished by prayer. We see over and over in the gospels that Jesus Himself modeled a solid prayer life (see Matthew 26:36; Mark 1:35; Luke 6:12; 9:28). In fact, Luke records that Jesus "often withdrew into the wilderness and prayed" (Luke 5:16).

Further, the book of Acts tells us that in the early Church "all continued with one accord in prayer and supplication" (Acts 1:14). We read the tangible results of that diligent, regular prayer:

- People prayed and miracles took place (see Acts 3:1–10).
- People prayed and new ministry was opened (see Acts 10:1–48).
- People prayed and the Body was strengthened in the midst of persecution (see Acts 4:23–31).
- People prayed and others were filled with the Spirit (see Acts 8:14–17).
- People prayed and saw visions from God (see Acts 22:17–18).
- People prayed when they were in desperate straits and got direction (see Acts 12:5–10).

The breath of Kingdom living has always been prayer, yet too often the devotional time—our daily time of being in His presence—gets crowded out. Now, as I considered the Lord's words to me, *You have forgotten the discipline of a daily devotional habit,* I realized I was being summoned back to renew the simplicity and intimacy of my earlier practice. That day something rekindled inside me, and I knew that Jesus was inviting me to a place where that "first love" with Him could be found again.

FIRST THINGS FIRST: SETTING THE "PRACTICALS" INTO PLACE

When I teach pastors, they will often ask how much time I spend in devotions each day. I always hesitate to answer that question because the answer can be so subjective. What is a lot for one person can be a little for another, and vice versa. Rather, I usually give a rule that I abide by: Set aside *time*, but not a specific *duration* of time. In other words, if you start by having to fill so many minutes or hours, you will defeat yourself right from the beginning. It will become a task rather than a point of entry into relationship with the living God.

Obviously, you will usually have to be finished by a certain time to get to work or other responsibilities of the day. But there are some days that my schedule allows me to spend more time than others; there are even days when my "business" with the Lord—the work in prayer that I needed to do—gets done more quickly. God is not counting our minutes every time we come before Him; He is meeting with us as dear children. As with our own children, sometimes that takes more time and sometimes it takes less. This is a relationship, not clocking in. The flexibility of leaving the length of time undefined allows us a freedom that a defined amount of time does not. So, have a set appointment with Jesus, but an undefined amount of time. If this is new for you, I would suggest starting with about fifteen minutes. But with the passing of time, you may find that you need to allow a little more time because *you want to*, not because someone says that you have to. If you abstain from setting a time goal it will never become a bondage to you; it will be a rejoicing to you.

I would further recommend adjusting your schedule in a way that practically allows you time in the morning. Over many years of walking with the Lord, I have discovered the wisdom of coming to Him at the beginning of a day to receive direction and guidance, rather than simply reviewing the day at its end. As I said, this may require some adjusting. You may need to set an earlier bedtime and let go of something that you might normally do in the evening. For instance, I used to stay up to watch the late night news. My time adjustment came by realizing that I would get the same information in less than half the time by checking the paper in the morning. That simple adjustment freed me from the need to stay up later, and, thereby, released time to spend with Jesus in the morning.

As we look at renewing our devotional time, we are going to explore four areas that can successfully shape a daily devotional prayer time. These are to:

1. Present yourself
2. Present your heart
3. Present your day
4. Present your "reach"

PRESENT YOURSELF

The best way I know to present yourself to the Lord is to come before Him with thanksgiving and praise. The Bible says, "Enter into His gates with thanksgiving, and into His courts with praise" (Psalm 100:4). Praise is always the entry point. Scripture further tells us that the Lord is "enthroned in the praises" of His people (Psalm 22:3). When we praise Him, we not only come into His presence, but also invite His rule into our lives and current situations.

Thank Him for who He is! He is our Savior, our help, our strong tower. He is our Lord, our provider, our guide. Require of yourself to say what that has meant in your life. Too often we say a phrase in praise and simply move on. It isn't that we do not mean it; but expanding the "why" of what we say, dwelling on what that means to us and elaborating it in His presence will cause praise to flow at greater dimensions.

Then thank the Lord for what He has done. The Bible tells us that His mercies are new every morning (see Lamentations 3:22–23), and every day there are things that happen in our lives that are only a result of the manifest grace of God. But without review, those gifts can slip by unnoticed. So each morning, go back and mentally review the preceding day, thanking Him for one situation where God's kindness was shown to you. Keep it current. Don't be living on the basis of historic things He has done. What did He do *yesterday*? We must always be watchful for His kindness, always thankful for His mercy. In fact, Nehemiah 9:17 teaches a significant concept. The chapter has described the Israelites' journey through the wilderness, along with their many bad attitudes: disobedience, pride, presumption, rebellion, thank-lessness. Verse 17 tells us that what allowed all of these attitudes to find a place in the hearts of the people was that they "were not mindful of [His] wonders." May that never be true of us. May His wonders be daily on our lips.

Another way to present yourself is in your physical stance of worship. Romans 12:1 instructs us to "present your bodies a living sacrifice, holy, acceptable to God, which is your reasonable worship."

How do you present your body as an act of worship? Traditionally, we think of kneeling. But it certainly is not the only way to present yourself to Him. The point is not to give a ritual performance; the point is submission of yourself before Him. Lift up your hands, lift up your head. It does not have to be the same thing every day. Read through the psalms and see how many different postures of worship there are and present your body to the Lord. Scripture talks about lifting your hands unto God as your source, standing in praise before your King, clapping your hands with rejoicing, dancing with childlike joy, bowing your head in humility, lifting your head with expectancy and prostrating yourself in dependency. Each day, you will find that the physical stance you use will reflect a different feeling of your heart and express in a different manner the hunger you have for the Lord.

Use of the tongue, that unruly member of the body, is an important aspect of thanksgiving and praise, as well as another way we present our body. In Psalm 96:1, David says, "Oh, sing to the LORD a new song!" That is a song that has never been sung before, and will probably never be sung again! Come before the Lord and be creative with your voice. Offer your own praise to the Lord; offer your own melody. Sing worship! In Ephesians 5:18 Paul says, "Be filled with the Spirit." The tense here implies continual action—that is, *keep on being filled* with the Spirit. Lift your voice. Employ spiritual utterance. Praise with the understanding, and praise with the Spirit.

PRESENT YOUR HEART

As you have presented yourself before the Lord with thanksgiving and praise, now present your heart to Him to be cleansed. Psalm 139 has verses that many of us are familiar with: "Search me, O God, and know my heart; try me, and know my anxieties; and see if there is any wicked way in me, and lead me in the way everlasting" (verses 23–24).

David's open door policy toward God teaches us a fundamental lesson: The purpose of having Him search our hearts is so we may discover sin and confess it. This kind of openness—confessing sin without self-justifying debate—allows the Lord free entry to examine and correct us. We accept His dealings and agree with His assessments. Baring our hearts before Him invites Him to point out blind spots, areas of unforgiveness, places where we are susceptible to the entangling of sin, or things in our hearts that are wrongly motivated. Coming to Him at the beginning of the day and having Him renew our awareness of where we need *His strength* is much better than coming to Him at the end of the day, beaten up because we tried to do it in our own strength.

I do not say this unkindly or with condemnation, but many people become tangled in sin that is ongoing in their lives, and they do not even recognize it until they start paying the penalty for it. Much of the time I have spent counseling people is simply helping them recognize where they pushed the wrong buttons— and they had no idea they were even leaning on them. It is very rare to talk with people who say they made up their minds to intentionally pursue sin. Rather it is because they have not developed the discipleship practice of asking the Lord to help them check for any "wicked" way that might be trying to linger in the shadows. Most people who have made a decision for Jesus Christ want to serve Him; but there is a place in our devotional time for daily "internal review."

Let me add that some people live under the notion that they can sin indiscriminately and the Lord is obligated to forgive. First let me just say, God is not *obligated* to do anything. The apostle Paul, in fact, strongly challenges this idea when he asks, "Shall we continue in sin that grace may abound? Certainly not!" (Romans 6:1–2). Moreover, God is calling us to learn how to grow beyond our own weaknesses, "as obedient children, not conforming yourselves to the former lusts, as in your ignorance; but as He who called you is holy, you also be holy in all *your* conduct, because it is written, 'Be holy, for I am holy' " (1 Peter 1:14–16, emphasis added). The way we live beyond it is to come to Him before we get caught in the weak places. We sometimes hesitate to acknowledge those places in our lives due to shame, embarrassment or condemnation. But just as someone would protect an injury—a weak place—we need to freely bring those things to Him, freely admitting in His presence that we cannot live our lives outside of His strength. We will still fail sometimes, but our sensitivity toward it will have changed radically, as well as the immediacy with which we deal with it.

When I was a boy, my dad always gave me a list of chores I was to do on Saturday morning before I could go and play. It would usually take all morning for me to do my chores. Then, later in the day, when he got home from work, he would take the list and go around with me and see how everything was done. For example, if my list included "sweep up the workshop in the basement," he might check the workshop and say, "Son, behind that leg of the workbench there's some sawdust you didn't get." I would clean that up, and when I was finished, he would say, "That's good work, son." Then the next week when I swept the workshop, no sawdust would be left behind the bench because now I knew what to look for. I had learned a new level of watchfulness.

In the same way, if we invite the Lord at the beginning of the day and ask Him to keep us undeceived, He will do it. If we let Him review our hearts and point out things, then we know to look for the sawdust behind the workbench. It's part of our training as sons and daughters. Then when something comes up, we can take care of it right then, and the blood of Jesus Christ will keep on cleansing us from all sin (see 1 John 1:7). Praise the Lord that it is an ongoing process! And we need it every day, as we are continually being formed into His image (see 2 Corinthians 3:18).

PRESENT YOUR DAY

To present your day to the Lord means, quite simply, mentioning all the things that your day holds. Psalm 5 reminds us to come each day: "Every morning I lay out the pieces of my life on your altar and watch for fire to descend" (Psalm 5:3, THE MESSAGE).

Not only are we offering the day as a sacrifice, but asking that His power and anointing come upon it as we seek to penetrate the darkness of our world with His fire.

This time also allows us to hear any adjustments that He may make in our day. Proverbs 3:6–7 says, "In all your ways acknowledge Him, and He shall direct your paths. Do not be wise in your own eyes; fear the LORD and depart from evil." *Being wise in your own eyes* does not mean being brash; it means thinking you can figure everything out. It means being self-sufficient. It means not being reliant on the Lord. The fact is that we cannot do anything apart from Him. Not one step; not one breath. Acknowledging our honest dependency is not resigning our own responsibilities as thoughtful, capable beings. Rather, it is the recognition that we have been made by Him, and we must be sustained by Him.

When my daughter was very suddenly widowed, she learned this lesson in a very practical way. That season, of course, carried with it incredible transition and intense emotion. Because of the turmoil of that season, each morning as she began to write down what she thought needed to be accomplished that day, she learned to listen very intently to the Lord's directions. Some days, He did not make any adjustments as she wrote her list in His presence. But other days He would be very explicit: *You aren't ready for that yet. Do this instead.* Each day was specifically directed by Him at a dimension unknown to her before. The Bible tells us, "Show me Your ways, O LORD; teach me Your paths. Lead me in Your truth and teach me, for You are the God of my salvation; on You I wait all the day" (Psalm 25:4–5). When we present our day to Him, and ask for His guidance, He will do just that. The book of James further adds, "If any of you lacks wisdom, let him ask of God, who gives to all liberally and without reproach, and it will be given to him" (James 1:5).

Our view will always be limited by our humanity, by our sin nature and by our ability to only see today. But Jesus is the Alpha and the Omega. He knows where we have been and He knows how to get us where He wants us to go. Our limited view can only provide us with, at best, an educated guess. But if we begin our days by listening for His instructions first, walking in obedience and staying connected to our Source, we will be able to proclaim with the words of the psalmist that our steps are ordered by the Lord (see Psalm 37:23).

PRESENT YOUR "REACH"

When it comes to presenting your "reach," I am talking about your influence. We all have influence in the lives of those around us, whether we think we do or not; and I would like for us to look at this concept in terms of ever-expanding circles of "family."

Of course, the obvious place to begin is with your immediate family, or your everyday circle of reach. You may no longer live with family, but there are those you have contact with every day—whether that is a roommate, friends or co-workers. The next circles include your extended family and friends, and your church family—the Father's family. And finally, the family circle will include the world—the human family. Luke writes that God "has made from one blood every nation of men to dwell on all the face of the earth" (Acts 17:26). This is also our family in the largest sense, and part of our prayer responsibility.

The Circle of Your Immediate Family

In the book of Job, we read that he prayed for his children every day. The Bible says that he would "rise early in the morning and offer burnt offerings according to the number of them all [his children]. . . . Thus Job did regularly" (Job 1:5).

It is obvious from this text that Job was deeply concerned about the welfare of his family before the Lord. And there is no reason to think that he did not pray for other family members besides his children. The life-changing thing about praying for our families is that, as we do, it will radically change our attitudes toward them. We are all tempted to pray for change in our family members; but what I have seen is that when people begin praying for their families, the Lord starts changing them! They begin to pray for a genuine, honest quest for understanding, for God's will in the life of each person and for them to reach their full potential in Him. How many marriages would be different if couples would begin to pray for one another? How many parent-child issues would be resolved? Maybe you do not have a spouse or children, but you do have a close, intimate circle of those you love. Name them before the Lord.

Anna and I learned the impact of this kind of prayer one Thanksgiving. We used to love to host Thanksgiving dinner. Now that kids and grandkids are married, Thanksgiving moves around more than it used to! But we would get extra tables and they would stretch around the corner of the dining room and down into the living room. When my dad was alive I would sit at one end and he would sit at the other end. And we had a tradition—it took almost the entire dinnertime, but we would go around the table and each person would relate a blessing of God in his or her life that year.

One year, my dad waited on purpose to talk last. He did not relate a blessing but, rather, he said, "I want to thank the Lord for the fact that all of you are living for the Lord and serving Him." And then he added, "I pray for all of you seven times a day." I was deeply moved to know that my dad took the time to pray for me, Anna, and each of our children *seven* times a day! And, I am deeply thankful for the heritage in Christ that my parents gave me. Praying parents have a remarkable influence over the destiny of their children.

As you read this, one of your children may be walking away from the Lord. Do not give in to hopelessness or despair. Begin to pray! Your children will come back to the Lord (see Jeremiah 31:17), but it comes about as parents pray. Grasp the truth of God's Word, and go to your knees.

The Circle of Your Extended Family

The next circle is described in Isaiah 58:7: "[Do] not hide yourself from your own flesh." When the Lord impressed those words upon me I knew He was teaching me something about loving those who get added to the family, or those who are more distantly related. I did not understand when I first got married that we need to love our in-laws as if they are our blood relatives. I never had a bad relationship with my in-laws, but, as a young man newly married, my attitude toward them was rather indifferent . . . until the Lord challenged me that this, too, was part of my family circle.

Anna comes from a large family—nine brothers and sisters! When I added in their spouses and children, then my siblings and their families, the number of names became unwieldy. Between our two families, and our own kids, we have well over eighty names! Yet, the Lord had given me this word about not hiding from my own flesh. So how do you pray for dozens of people on a daily basis? Not only would naming eighty names every day start to feel like "vain repetition," but you would burn out inside of two weeks.

First, Scripture makes clear that the naming of names—or carrying those names before the Lord—is of significance. When the priests of Israel went into the Temple, their garments had engraved stones that simply had the names of all of the tribes of Israel on them. Scripture tells us that in this way, the priest would "bear their names before the LORD on his two shoulders as a memorial" (Exodus 28:12); and that he would "bear the judgment of the children of Israel over his heart before the LORD continually" (Exodus 28:30). In the names of the tribes that were engraved, the entire nation was represented. Every person in Israel could trace his or her lineage back to one of those twelve names. When "naming the names" gets wearisome, remember we are called to bear those names both on our shoulders and over our hearts.

But a workable solution that I have found is to name the names within my reach in cycles. Bring your most intimate circle before the Lord daily, but spread out the list of extended family members over a more extended period of time so that you are sure you are not leaving anyone out.

The Circle of Your Church Family

In Ephesians 3:14–15 Paul says, "I bow my knees to the Father of our Lord Jesus Christ, from whom the whole family in heaven and earth is named." That family is all who name the name of Jesus Christ as Savior—the Church. Scripture makes clear that we have been adopted into the family of God with Him as our Father (see Galatians 4:6). As surely as we are called to pray for our earthly, biological family, we are called to lift our spiritual family before the Lord. Scripture tells us that one goal of our Adversary, the devil, is to "wear out the saints" (Daniel 7:25, KJV). That fact alone should keep us on our knees for one another.

Start by naming your pastor and his or her family before the Lord daily. Can I encourage you never to pray for your pastor without also praying for his or her spouse? God has made them one, and because they are one, they bear this ministry together.

Then name other pastors who minister in your city. Scripture says that those in ministry carry a greater burden before the Lord because they will have to answer for how they have shepherded the flock of God (see Hebrews 13:17; 1 Peter 5:2). It is a joyous burden to bear, but comes with greater accountability before the Father.

Pray for people in your congregation you know who are sick or facing difficulties with their jobs, their families or their marriages. Pray for young people as they face the challenges of living a godly life in an increasingly perverse society. Pray for relationships to be strong. Pray for promises of the Father to be released in the lives of brothers and sisters in Christ. The Bible tells us to "bear one another's burdens, and so fulfill the law of Christ" (Galatians 6:2). Ask the Lord to bring people to mind, and then pray for them. We don't know what heartbreaks and challenges people are facing. The apostle Paul writes that we are to "pray without ceasing" (1 Thessalonians 5:17). One way the Lord helps us to do that is to remind us of people so we can pray for them.

Include the solitary in your list of names. That phrase *the solitary* comes from Psalm 68:6: "God sets the solitary in families." Ask the Lord to help you see "the alone one" so that you can draw him or her in. For many, life circumstances have left them alone through death or divorce, dysfunction or broken dreams. Begin by adopting them in prayer; then let the Lord show you ways to help draw them in to the family. He wants to put the solitary in families, and will show you for whom to pray.

The Circle of the Human Family

Psalm 2:8 says, "Ask of Me, and I will give You the nations for Your inheritance, and the ends of the earth for Your possession." This passage is not talking about reinstituting colonization; it is talking about redemption. It is an Old Testament reference to what would become the Church's commission: "You shall be witnesses to Me in Jerusalem, and in all Judea and Samaria, and to the end of the earth" (Acts 1:8).

The concept of bringing "the nations" before the Lord in prayer can seem like a daunting task, but there are several guidelines that I have found can help. First, many people have found great benefit in using a calendar or planner. Different countries can be listed by months or days as prayer reminders. As mentioned above in praying for extensive lists of names, a planner can help you to list in cycles the people and nations you want to pray for. You may want to pray through all of the countries of the world, or you may want to focus on a specific continent.

A second guideline is to make use of an atlas. When I open my atlas and look at a country, I begin to see that nation as more than just a "word." I begin to see cities and towns; I see divisions of a nation, such as states, districts, territories and provinces. I begin to get a feel for the fact that this is not just the name of a particular piece of land, but it is the name of *a people*.

On the news, I may hear something about a country—a disaster, economic challenge or political upheaval. Knowing where that country is located and the nations surrounding it helps me to target whole areas in prayer. In the wake of upheaval, there are often opportunities for the spread of the Gospel, and hearts that are softened to respond.

In the realm of the Spirit of God, I begin to recognize I am doing more than reciting names or situations to Almighty God, but by the power of His Holy Spirit working in me—a redeemed human being—according to the promises of God's Word, I am interceding for an entire people, and He begins to work to give us "the nations as an inheritance." Make no mistake, we are extending the reach and dominion of God's Kingdom as surely as Adam and Eve were originally called to; as surely as the Church is now called to extend the Gospel into every nation. We are planting seeds in the spiritual realm that will grow unto harvest (see 1 Corinthians 3:6–8).

Never doubt that we are making a difference in prayer! We are sometimes tempted to pray as though we think God is arbitrary; as though He *says* He gives us privilege and authority in prayer, but really just goes around doing what He wants to. Nothing could be further from the truth! Scripture has recorded what He says: "Ask of Me, and I *will* give you the nations" (Psalm 2:8, emphasis added); "If My people who are called by My name will humble themselves, and pray . . . I *will* hear" (2 Chronicles 7:14, emphasis added).

We need to challenge the heresy that exists unchallenged in the subconscious of many Christians that "what will be will be." As sons and daughters of the living God, we need to come to grips with that false idea of predestined fate. Even though things and people may be redeemed, they are not redeemed without someone stepping in. Jesus stepped in to redeem us unto salvation; then through His cross He released us to step into our world, offering His redemption and life to the ends of the earth.

KEEP PRESSING IN!

While you are learning, keep pressing forward, and never let the liar discourage your spirit. We can be tempted to think about daily prayer the same way that we do New Year's resolutions. We get excited about the newness of what the Lord is working in our lives, and pray three days in a row. Then something comes up and we miss a day. If we miss two more days, we feel as though we are back down to zero again! It is as if we were scoring points and now we are behind. That is absolutely a lie of the devil. When we miss a day, all that happens is that we missed a day; it does not annul the days when we did pray.

Learning the habit of daily devotional prayer will take time. But it is step one in learning to penetrate the darkness through prayer. As growing disciples, we build that foundation of daily prayer. But there will also be times that the Lord calls us to deeper dimensions of prayer. Scripture talks about other kinds of prayer through which we can extend the light and life of His Kingdom.

4

INTERCESSION 101

The Spirit Himself makes intercession for us with groanings
which cannot be uttered. Now He who searches the hearts
knows what the mind of the Spirit is, because He makes
intercession for the saints according to the will of God.

ROMANS 8:26– 27

Recent years have brought the beginning of a deeper grasp of inter-cessory prayer throughout many parts of the Body of Christ. But there are many who yet perceive *intercession* simply as a synonym for *prayer*. This is unsurprising since many dictionaries commonly contribute to this limited perspective. Thereby, *intercession* along with *supplication*—another Bible word with distinct dynamic of meaning—are often used or read as *alternative words* for prayer rather than dimensions of *applied prayer*. The richness of meaning and practical integration of intercession as a conscious approach in prayer unfolds truth I have found to be clarifying and motivat-ing in the lives of believers. Just as truth sets us free from sin and death, truth related to prayer can unleash new boldness and faith with confidence and joy.

THE TERM IN SCRIPTURE

Years ago, one of my college professors gave some very wise counsel about understanding Scripture. He said, "If you don't know what a word means, the best commentary you can find on the Bible is the Bible. If you want to know what the Holy Spirit intends when He uses a word, find out how He uses the word other places."

Taking this advice, I began to study the word *intercession* and its usage throughout Scripture, as well as looking at it in the original languages Scripture was written in. I discovered that there are several definitions. The first was: "To light upon a person or a thing, to fall in with, to hit upon a person or a thing." In other words the idea of intercession meant to chance upon something, or to encounter something unexpectedly.

Quite frankly, I was puzzled by this definition. I thought, *Intercession? To encounter unexpectedly?* That kind of happenstance in prayer did not compute. It did not seem likely to me that the Lord would say, "I want you to pray accidentally or when the idea strikes you."

A bit mystified, I moved to the second definition. That one read: "To meet a person, especially for conversation or a consultation." That made sense. It is easy to see how intercession has to do with entering into counsel with the eternal Father, particularly to seek guidance from Him about the needs of another person or situation. That was easier to understand.

What really caught my attention and got me thinking, though, was that first definition, because it was the definition of primary usage; yet, it sounded kind of like serendipity, something we would not expect, something that just sort of . . . happens.

Continued study showed that in the Old Testament, the Hebrew word for *intercession* occurs about fifty times. The word

is *pagah* and means "to impinge, by accident or by violence."
Impinge can be defined as "to encroach or to advance beyond
the usual limit." Immediately evident in these definitions is the
concept of taking territory, of forward movement, of pressing
into. These definitions lead us directly into a deeper awareness
of what the Bible really means when it speaks of penetrating the
darkness, shaking up the spiritual realm and seeing the Kingdom
come through intercession.

ENLARGING THE BORDERS

The first definition we are going to look at is "advancing
beyond the usual limit." This use of the word occurs often in the
book of Numbers when Israel's boundaries were being allocated
by the Lord, and tribal boundaries assigned. Before His people
entered "the land"—the Promised Land that had been covenanted
generations before to Israel's ancestors—God gave them direction
as to how their boundaries should be laid out. They already had
a basic understanding of the land, because years before they had
sent the twelve spies in to study the area. The Lord appointed
a distinct inheritance for each of the twelve tribes, and then for
each family within a tribe.

The Lord is so specific here with His people that we need to
keep in mind the personal significance that just as God ordained
boundaries for the tribes and the families of Israel, so He has determined boundaries for your life and mine. This is what David meant
in Psalm 16:5–6 when he wrote: "O LORD, You are the portion of
my inheritance and my cup; You maintain my lot. The lines have
fallen to me in pleasant places; yes, I have a good inheritance."

In these verses, David describes his "good inheritance" from
the Lord: He is the Source (*You are my portion*); He is the One
who defines the inheritance (*You maintain my lot);* and He has

determined the "quality" of what He intends for us to have (*pleasant, good inheritance*). God has determined your lot, your inheritance. This concept is even applied to God's sovereign purposes for nations. When Paul was preaching to the philosophers on Mars Hill, he said that God has determined where the boundaries of mankind's habitation should fall (see Acts 17:26). So in the light of these references it should not surprise us that in regard to us as the Lord's redeemed, Ephesians 1:11–12 would further mention our inheritance in Him:

> In Him also we have obtained an inheritance, being predestined according to the purpose of Him who works all things according to the counsel of His will, that we who first trusted in Christ should be to the praise of His glory.

It applies to each person who opens to God's Kingdom purposes—its intention to assure the inheritance, or purpose, God has in His plan for our lives.

Scripture also makes clear that He sees something in you and He sees something in me that excites Him—something of life and purpose for you that is the reason He called you to Himself. The apostle Paul prays that "the eyes of your understanding [may be] enlightened; that you may know what is the hope of His calling, what are the riches of the glory of His inheritance in the saints" (Ephesians 1:18), and that we may "lay hold of that for which Christ Jesus has also laid hold of [us]" (Philippians 3:12).

He sees the boundaries of possibility in us. He "laid hold" of each of us for a reason! You may sometimes wonder about your own life. There are times when every one of us feels that our lives are constricted or limited by circumstances. "Is this it? Is this all there is?" we ask. But the concept of intercession carries with it the possibility of boundaries pressed to what was intended to be. The redemption we have in Jesus Christ provides not just "covering" for our sin and failure, but "recovering" His intended boundaries. No matter what you face today of limitation, there is always hope for recovering God's original boundaries of your life. The challenge for us is that rarely do we ever reach the limit of our boundaries, let alone begin to enlarge them.

The term *intercession* occurs about eight times in this sense, indicating that the Israelites would come to a place where they had brought under their dominion the originally established boundary that God intended; but now, that boundary needed to be fully established to secure the fruitfulness and fulfillment of all that the Lord had originally planned for them. (We see this usage of the word most often in Joshua 19, when the boundaries are described as reaching a prescribed limit.)

This is the same word-root, *pagah*, that is used in Isaiah 59:16 when the Lord wondered that there was no intercessor. In other words, in this definition, the boundary is to be *interceded into*. The intercessor follows God's plan and purpose to bring about His will of enlargement. The boundary will never reach its full extent unless it is interceded into. While the Israelites had their boundaries assigned, the land itself was still unconquered. Though God had defined a set of boundaries for each person, it was left to the individual to press into them . . . to intercede into them.

God's boundaries for us are never limiting. Where we find ourselves today, or where we see a family member struggling, or where we see a co-worker held back—these are never the extent of what the Lord has for any one of us! He has called us to enlargement in every dimension of life, but that comes by pressing into, by recovering the covenanted boundaries through intercession. In our lives, and the lives of those around us, boundaries can be reduced through debt, death, sin or assault of the enemy. Indeed, we see this in Israel's history, where land could be turned over to pay a debt (see Leviticus 25:24–28), or death caused land to go into another's hands (see Numbers 27). Israel repeatedly saw their own boundaries constricted through their own pursuit of sin and idolatry (the book of Judges shows this repeated cycle). These boundaries were never recovered without intentional action—redemptively on God's part, and through "interceding into" on the part of the people. The same is true in the lives of God's people today. Just as Israel had to intercede into larger boundaries by conquering the enemy, we are called to press back the assault of the Adversary and extend—intercede into—larger boundaries, penetrating the darkness and taking new ground for God's Kingdom.

None of this is to suggest that either these texts or anything else in God's Word directs us to "instruct" God as to what we want or to even imagine it is our right to require Him to do something or satisfy what we think best. Rather intercession—in every expression—is that prayer privilege that refuses to yield to the limits that so often confine or reduce.

"FALLING UPON THE ENEMY"

The Hebrew definition of *intercession* also carries the concept of extending by violence or by battle. In this case, *intercession* is translated "to fall upon," as soldiers do in battle. It obviously links conceptually to the previous definition of extending boundaries and taking territory, when warfare is required for the full extension of God's intended boundaries of blessing for people.

The primary example of this usage is from a very negative circumstance in Scripture. First Samuel 22:6–23 tells us of the time that King Saul, blinded by his jealousy of David, commanded some of his soldiers to kill certain priests of Israel who had innocently aided the young man. The soldiers would not comply because they respected the Lord, His ways and those who served Him. They were willing to incur the wrath of their king rather than disobey the word of the Lord.

When they would not obey him, Saul turned to another one of his soldiers, an Edomite named Doeg. As a foreigner and a mercenary enlisted by Saul, Doeg had no such compunctions as Israel's soldiers had. His loyalty was to Saul and Saul alone. Saul told Doeg to kill the priests, and with the approval of the king, Scripture tells us that Doeg "fell upon" the priests of the Lord, and killed 85 of them that day; and here, "fell upon" translates the verb *pagah*.

Though this example of *pagah* is set in a negative context, it still presents a key lesson in the use of intercessory prayer. As we intercede, we are "falling upon" the Adversary to see God's will done upon the earth. While Doeg's actions wickedly achieved a wayward king's will, we are called to war "against principalities, against powers, against the rulers of the darkness of this age, against spiritual hosts of wickedness in the heavenly places" (Ephesians 6:12). Those words direct a striking down of evil forces to see God's love and mercy and grace extended into people's lives.

MEETING UNEXPECTEDLY

The third meaning of *intercede* is responding to a situation you have "chanced upon," and this is the definition that baffled me at first. In Genesis 27:41-45, Jacob was running for his life from his brother, Esau. Jacob had already deceived his father and deceptively connived a means to take their father Isaac's paternal blessing from his brother. In anger, Esau pursued his brother, and Jacob did well to run.

Though Jacob had certainly not possessed the blessing in a righteous way, the family shared a belief in God that Jacob embraced, and which Esau despised. Jacob's "style" at this point—one in which God's grace overcomes his immaturity—is a prompter to consider, regarding ourselves. How many of us, having begun our lives with the Lord, may be like Jacob? We believe . . . yet the discipleship process has yet to begin. Jacob had a long way to go to become the man that God wanted him to be, but that does not mean that God was not at work in bringing Jacob to His purpose. Thank the Lord, He does that with all of us! He is always leading us toward His purpose for us.

Looking now into Jacob's encounter with God, we find him running for his life because of his own scheming. The Bible says that as Jacob was running he "lighted upon a certain place" (Genesis 28:11, KJV). He decided that was as far as he would go that night, pulled up a few rocks and laid his head down on them. This is the place where, before the night was over, he would have a vision of angels ascending and descending a ladder that reached to heaven. This term *lighted upon a certain place* is *pagah*—our word *intercession*—and is used here in the sense of "happening upon" a place, a place where God has arranged "an appointment," a place when God's purpose is understood and responded to.

Jacob's "chance encounter" resulted in his calling the place Bethel, "house of God." Though this was an unplanned stop, it turned out to be the place of God's revealed will. What a great picture of God's "waking us up" to a situation where He seeks to introduce His Kingdom—His will on earth as it is in heaven. He may alert us to a prayer assignment, place us in an unplanned moment for ministry to someone or stop us in an encounter with Himself regarding His purposes for our own lives.

APPLYING THE "PAGAH" LESSONS

I cannot remember when I have been more deeply moved in understanding the privilege and responsibility we have in prayer than I was as I studied the meaning of this word, its various uses and their practical implications. The three settings in which *pagah* is used present a broad significance in the Word, giving us examples of intercession in order (1) to see the boundaries of God's Kingdom intentions extend as far as they were meant to reach; (2) to direct prayer as an executing of God's justice against evil according to His Kingdom's order; and (3) to respond in a place of prayer that you have chanced upon unexpectedly. Now let's look at these and probe deeper at how this may be lived out in our lives.

One: Extending Our Boundaries

The intercessor is one who may, through Christ's victory applied by faith in prayer, establish and extend boundaries to see heaven's will established on earth. Perhaps the best definition of *intercession* according to the Word of God is to describe the intercessor as "one who stands before God on behalf of persons or situations that either cannot or will not come before God on their own."

The most dramatic evidence we could possibly be given is that the verb *pagah* is used of Jesus—the Messiah Himself—as prophesied in Isaiah 53:12. This precious passage, which in verse 5 describes Jesus' suffering for our salvation, includes in verse 12 a description of our Savior standing—making intercession—before God for us:

But He was wounded for our transgressions, He was bruised for our iniquities; the chastisement for our peace was upon

59

Him, and by His stripes we are healed. . . . By His knowledge My righteous Servant shall justify many, for He shall
bear their iniquities . . . because He poured out His soul
unto death, and He was numbered with the transgressors,
and He bore the sin of many, and made intercession for the
transgressors.

ISAIAH 53:5, 11–12

How magnificently and conclusively our Lord Jesus Christ is
displayed as the ultimate Intercessor! And how clearly and beauti-
fully we see Jesus as our pattern—standing before God on our
behalf when we neither would nor could ever come before God
on our own!

So it is that His cross introduces God's grand recovery program:
to redeem and restore on earth everything that was lost through
man's Fall. That victory is applied as believers today intercede—to
stand in, to contend in prayer—that the victory of Christ may be
applied here as it has been secured in heaven.

The boundaries lost by Adam and Eve's sins are now available
to be extended again to God's intent in the lives of multitudes—all
through the cross as the Church intercedes and bears witness of
all that Jesus has done for us. When you and I offer the place of
rulership in our lives to God, He not only begins to work in us,
but He intends to make us agents of His Kingdom, reclaiming
the role that men and women were originally created to fill. He
is calling us to become instruments of redemption—instruments
of interceding into the intended boundaries.

The same recovery of boundaries certainly applied to you
and me when we came to Christ. We see examples of this in
our own lives. When we were trapped in the prison of our own
shame, bound by the cords of iniquity, leashed by the Adversary who dragged us along, chained and bound, we heard the

message of liberty through One who hung upon His cross in our place.

When we were like sheep gone astray, God laid on Him—interceded through Him—for us all. The chastisement of our peace was upon Him and by His stripes we are healed. Because of Jesus' work on the cross the boundaries of our lives have been extended. The leash has been snapped, the chains were broken and we have been released to move into the purposes of God.

Do you see the picture? Can you realize the full extent of what Jesus accomplished that day at Calvary? Sickness, disease, heartache—all these things continually erode God's intended boundaries for every person. Instead of living on a continent of blessing, people end up standing on a little island, afraid to move. The tides of darkness have eaten away at God's intended large place for them.

Not only was our inheritance opened to us through the Lord's intercession, but this instrument of prayer became available to us as well to advance His victory. When we see darkness pressing down and crowding circumstances, we can intercede in the name of Jesus—because it is only in His name and by His blood that hell has to yield.

> God also has . . . given Him the name which is above every name, that at the name of Jesus every knee should bow, of those in heaven, and of those on earth, and of those under the earth, and that every tongue should confess that Jesus Christ is Lord, to the glory of God the Father.
>
> PHILIPPIANS 2:9–11

This breaks down the walls the enemy has erected and presses back the encroaching darkness. Whatever the need—sickness, marital strife, provision, personal discord, mental anguish—we can come before the Father and intercede. The plan that God has in heaven is then worked out on earth because His people are willing to accept full access to all He has provided. His people are able to intercede because He has interceded for us. His people are ready to extend the boundaries of His Kingdom to their fullest extent.

Two: Justice at the King's Command

The second idea of intercession as a matter of executing judgment and justice is fairly easily understood. We have already looked at its usage in Scripture and the evil nature of the actions of Doeg. But if we can look beyond the evil of that moment, we can see that basically he was executing the will of the king. That "falling upon" describes intercession, and what we are called to do. It is offensive—not defensive—action, militarily speaking.

It is by *falling upon*—with faith and the sword of the Spirit—that we strike down the enemy. This is precisely what Jesus was describing in Matthew 11:12: "From the days of John the Baptist until now the kingdom of heaven suffers violence, and the violent take it by force." How are we to comprehend Jesus' meaning in the words *the violent take the Kingdom by force?*

The word *biastai* is used in this text—the word describing "force or seizure." It is, however, describing something of the violence when "life is entering" into a situation. This concept is perhaps best illustrated in the force with which a woman's travail has come upon her, and the breakthrough that comes as a child is born from one world into another—the realm of the womb into a realm of vastly greater dimensions. *Biastai* derives from *bios*—the word from which we draw the English *biology*, the study of life on earth. Probably few words could better describe the life-giving vitality, energy and possibilities that come when the people of God intercede with the Spirit's power. The result is the birthing of souls from the constricting dimensions of this present world into the limitless and eternal possibilities of the Kingdom of God.

The Scriptures illustrate the travail of an intercessor praying with passion with a woman caught up in labor of childbirth (see Galatians 4:19). Such intercessory travail will be discussed later, but its life-giving power is not generated by human energy. It is entirely the result of the overflow of the Holy Spirit's power, welcomed by our openness to His fullness, and applied in times of earnest prayer. This is what Jesus meant when He said that out of our innermost beings would flow rivers of living water (see John 7:38). We have all seen what the water-force of a river can do. It is as though the Holy Spirit is flowing life into each of His sons and daughters in such a way that it begins to pour through us to multiply the life and prevailing work of God's Kingdom.

Three: Chance Encounters

Applying the third use of *pagah*, which we studied, introduces a solid reminder of how much Jesus has accomplished, and how little we bring to the situation in our own strength. Jacob's weakness and God's strength prompt a focus on the fact that everything pertaining to the work of the Lord in your life or mine is accomplished entirely by His power, unto His glory, through His cross. Still, this does not negate the fact that God reigns supremely, but shows that He also specifically calls us to partnership and growth in obedience to the ministry of intercession. His will is that we be involved in His purposes; we must be about the Father's business! We need to respond to what He shows us to do. But abiding faith and patience in pursuing patterns of intercession will only be sustained with durability as we always make our stand in the power of the Spirit and with the banner of the cross.

Wisdom will avoid the practice of some believers who start out strong, but somewhere along the line lose their focus. They become impressed with the power that they have been given over the enemy, rather than the *Source* of that power. The disciples did this one day, when they came to Jesus exclaiming, "Even the demons are subject to us!" Jesus' reminder was to "glory" not in the power they were given, but in the derivation of that power:

> Then the seventy returned with joy, saying, "Lord, even the demons are subject to us in Your name." And He said to them, "I saw Satan fall like lightning from heaven. Behold, I give you the authority to trample on serpents and scorpions, and over all the power of the enemy, and nothing shall by any means hurt you. Nevertheless do not rejoice in this, that the spirits are subject to you, but rather rejoice because your names are written in heaven."
>
> Luke 10:17–20

Our authority is derived from the fact that *through Jesus' blood, death and resurrection victory* our names are written in the Lamb's book of life. It is important to move in boldness against the Adversary; but it is of foremost importance to remember that this authority is all because of Christ's victory at Calvary.

PUTTING IT ALL TOGETHER

Let's use the metaphor of archers to understand how these three definitions of *intercession* all come together. The Bible says that God "covers His hands with lightning, and commands it to strike" (Job 36:32). Those willing to intercede are like arrows, bright as bolts of lightning, ready for His command.

God looks over His Kingdom and sees darkness that needs to be shattered, power that needs to enter into the confusion of human weakness. He calls us to intercession: See the picture of our prayers penetrating the darkness like bright arrows, hitting the mark as they extend the boundaries and purposes of God! The picture before us is not one of the Living God, like an ancient pagan deity reigning on high and looking for people to nail with lightning bolts! Rather, here is a powerful depiction of the Almighty God of the universe, seated on His throne and seeing demonic powers that are tormenting, afflicting and holding people in bondage. He begins moving His people by His Spirit of power to smite down dark spiritual powers.

In these days of upheaval in our world, of moral decay and increased uncertainty at every hand, the Lord is calling intercessors. Isaiah 59:14–19 says:

> Justice is turned back, and righteousness stands afar off; for truth is fallen in the street, and equity cannot enter. So truth fails, and he who departs from evil makes himself a prey. Then the LORD saw it, and it displeased Him that there was no justice. He saw that there was no man, and wondered that there was no intercessor; therefore His own arm brought salvation for Him; and His own righteousness, it sustained Him. For He put on righteousness as a breastplate, and a helmet of salvation on His head; He put on the garments of vengeance for clothing, and was clad with zeal as a cloak. According to their deeds, accordingly He will repay, fury to His adversaries, recompense to His enemies. So shall they fear the name of the LORD from the west, and His glory from the rising of the sun; when the enemy comes in like a flood, the Spirit of the LORD will lift up a standard against him.

In the face of decadent times, God—by His Spirit—moves to raise up warriors whose intercession prayerfully welcomes "on earth" His power to turn the Adversary back as prayer "lifts up a standard against him."

And He is looking for us to join Him today! Until the day Jesus comes, until His foot lands here and this world becomes His possession, until that glorious return, He calls His Church to penetrate the darkness by extending particular boundaries

> *. . . at His command*
> *. . . with His guidance*
> *. . . through the power of His cross.*

This is true intercession, and we learn more of its application and scope in the next chapter.

5

INTERCESSION PRACTICUM

I exhort first of all that supplications, prayers, intercessions,
and giving of thanks be made for all men.

1 TIMOTHY 2:1

A little five-year-old in our church was learning to pray, and she had decided she would pray that her grandfather would stop smoking. She had seen enough TV ads about the dangers of smoking, and had heard her parents express their concern over the habit, that she decided this would be something important to pray for. So, her little five-year-old heart accompanied by her five-year-old diligence prayed daily for her grandpa.

Until the next time she went for a visit.

She walked out on the patio and discovered Grandpa smoking, and in dismay informed him, "Well, if you aren't going to try to stop, I'm going to quit praying for you!"

We can chuckle at a five-year-old's response. But, similarly, a woman in our congregation once complained that she had prayed for the salvation of her extended family for six months and they had not gotten saved yet. "So is it okay if I stop praying?" she queried. In light of what we have learned so far about prayer and our diligence in it, the question seems ludicrous. That response in an adult can even seem rather immature, spiritually speaking. Yet we have all faced weariness in prayer and been tempted to stop when we don't get the answer we want, or the answer seems long in coming.

These examples serve only to point out the fact that stepping into the discipline of intercession requires something more of us. We have already acknowledged that intercession is a different kind of praying than our devotional prayer time with the Lord each day. But the *doing* of intercession requires that we:

1. Understand what we are seeking to accomplish in prayer
2. Learn how to hear the voice of the Lord
3. Respond in obedience to His promptings
4. Know our place in partnership
5. Make the long-term commitment to intercede for people and circumstances

The awesome power and potential of the intercessor is within the grasp of every believer, yet so few take it. In intercession we come to a realm of prayer that begins to reach out further than most people either realize they have the privilege of accomplishing or feel comfortable with. The very breadth of possibility can make it easy to become overwhelmed.

We also know our own limitations. While the Lord has called us to this glorious partnership with Him, we have to acknowledge that, basically, there is no way to cover all the needs we become aware of in the world around us in a day's time . . . or a week's time. Not only is time an issue, but in some cases, as we have already noted, naming long lists of people and places in our daily devotional habit would become tedious. Reciting lists of concerns that the Lord impresses on us soon becomes what Jesus said is impractical and of little value: Empty repetition does not accomplish anything (see Matthew 6:7).

In this calling of Scripture to offer sensitive, responsible prayers for people and issues, nations and circumstances beyond our scope (see Matthew 6:5-14; Mark 13:33; Luke 21:36), how do we put it all together? How do we find practical ways of accomplishing the challenges of intercession? How do we work in conjunction with the Holy Spirit to be instruments of redemption? How do we pray "on target"? How do we know what is His will when we pray?

In my years of instruction on the subject, I have found three points and three words that not only answer these questions, but also often help people grasp the partnership role the Lord has given us in intercession.

THREE POINTS TO UNDERSTAND

First, *intercession has to do with praying for somebody else.* The "somebody" may be a nation, someone you know or someone you do not know. It can be a family member or your congregation. Intercession has to do with *praying on behalf of.*

Second, *intercession relies on the Holy Spirit's guidance and help.* Romans 8:26–27 says that when the intercessor reaches the point that he or she does not know for sure what to pray, the Holy Spirit will help—will enable—prayer beyond what the intercessor knows or understands. He will also prompt us, reminding us of people or circumstances that need to be carried in intercessory prayer.

But relying on the Holy Spirit goes further than simply letting Him enable our prayer; it also requires us to listen for, hear and obey His voice as never before. The Lord has things to say to His people; He calls us to prayer and instructs us of things to pray for. A person will come to mind: a sense of need and urgency. The summons is to prayer, recognizing that all consequences depend upon it.

The Bible calls this "discernment" or "the word of wisdom" (1 Corinthians 12:8). It is another way He shows us how to pray for His will to be done on earth as it is in heaven. For any whom this concept makes nervous, let me briefly say here that the Holy Spirit and His working in our lives is never intended to be "weird." We only have to look as far as the life of Jesus to see that. He was bold in how He approached the workings of darkness, and He has poured out that same power on His Church. Jesus said that He only did what He saw the Father do (see John 5:19), and that same ability to see into the invisible realm has been given to us—His Body, the Church. We are called to be bold; we are called to see the invisible. We are also called to listen for His voice because He has things to tell us; and we are called to respond in prayer.

Third, *intercession challenges humankind's helplessness to deal with the largest issues of life.* We have already discussed our obvious inability to effect change in our lives or in the world outside of what Jesus has accomplished for us on the cross. At the same time, however, there is woven into the fabric of humankind a sense of powerlessness that cripples many, obstructing faith on the supposition that the issues of this world have been "predestined"—that is, already decided: The die is cast and a cosmic arrangement of things is fixed in place. What satanic darkness has structured and the things that human self-will and sinning have bound over to the will of flesh and the devil—so much of what we see around us—seems so firmly entrenched that we are tempted to feel that the best we can do is try to cope with it.

Jesus taught exactly the opposite. There is nothing in the Bible that suggests we are victims of unyielding circumstance. The whole concept of salvation argues against that: Christ's coming, reconciling us with the Father, reversing the death process by His resurrection—all of these are statements to us by the Father that nothing is beyond redemption. Nothing in your life, nothing in my life, nothing of anything we face— *nothing* is beyond redemption. But there is a decisive issue to be settled.

Where can our conquering Savior find, among those who have acknowledged Him as the Christ, the Son of the living God, those who will then *accept and apply the keys of the Kingdom*? Those keys, which represent the authority He is inviting us to exercise, constitute the key component to change. *Redemption on earth* advances as God's praying people take action, invoking through intercession the victory that is established *in heaven*.

So much of the Church lives passively, rather than taking action and becoming redemptive agents of God's Kingdom in our world. We are called to transmit through prayer the invitation: "Let Your Kingdom come! Enter into this circumstance, that problem, that soul, that home! Let your will be done in *our* family, *our* town, *our* nation—exactly as You, Father, will it in heaven. Release it in Jesus' name. Shed forth the blessing of His victory—apply what He has 'finished'!"

We are not called to live out fate, neither have we been appointed to walk in futility. With new birth, God has made possible growing sons and daughters, not robots, puppets or pawns. And He is calling us to take action—to partner, to step up, to take our place. He has made us agents and ambassadors, "joint heirs with Christ" (Romans 8:17) to extend His Son's Kingdom unto His praise and glory!

THREE WORDS TO DEFINE

The scope of this intercessory privilege can be summed up in three words: *intersection, intervention* and *interception*. Let's look at each one to see how it defines and broadens our understanding of the action we can take to penetrate the darkness of our world.

Intersection

The first word is *intersection*. This word is used in the sense you might expect: a crossing of two roads. You may know of a person facing a difficult choice, or co-workers who are deciding what they will choose regarding salvation. There may be a major vote in the state where you live, or the possibility of layoffs where you work. All of these examples represent people or circumstances coming to a crucial moment—a decision point—and what is brought to bear upon that moment in prayer determines which way things go. The intercessor's privilege is to bring to that crossroads, to that issue, what Christ has accomplished at the cross. And make no mistake: Just because we may not get the answer we want does not mean that God is not at work. His ways are above ours (see Isaiah 55:8). He is answering based on far more knowledge than ours, and He knows how all of the pieces are going to come together at the end. Never despair when things don't look like what you hoped. The sovereign Lord of the universe is still at work.

This is not rationalizing or theologizing; it is not figuring out a way to feel good about however our prayers turn out. Neither is it a means to make excuses for God. We are not called to "cover" for God; we are called to pray in faith. When my children were young, many of my decisions did not make sense to them in the moment, but later they understood. They understood that I saw more than they did, and that there were more pieces to fit together. They understood that my decisions were always, ultimately, for their best interests. And they learned to trust. Things may not always look the way we hoped, but we can always trust in our Father's workings. As surely as Christ on the cross did not "look like" what Israel expected, God was in action—accomplishing His bigger purposes. Two things took place when Jesus died:

First, He bore the beating of His own body in order to absorb into Himself the power of everything that breaks human life— spirit, soul and body. Sin, sickness, mental torment, failure, depression and all manner of evil have been absorbed by Him. Jesus took *all of it* upon Himself. So often we think in terms of Jesus taking "sin" on Himself. Of course we know that everything about our world that is broken is broken because of sin; but the use of the word can keep us disconnected from everything Jesus actually accomplished at the cross. This week alone I have encountered a girl facing a disability, a young man wrestling through a romantic breakup, a woman whose brother just committed suicide and a man who has had a major surgery. Not to mention people dealing with the impact of addictions, abuse, injustice, condemnation, hope miscarried, depression, worthlessness. All of these are the result of sin. And Jesus took all of it—*all of it*—upon Himself.

The second thing that took place at the cross is that hell was brought to its knees. Colossians 2:15 says that Jesus "disarmed principalities and powers" and "made a public spectacle of them, triumphing over them in it." Through His death Jesus divested all powers of hell of their capacity to sustain their program whenever they are confronted by the power of His cross. Hell knows that it is defeated, that this is a lost cause. Yet our Adversary has not given up the fight; we still face warfare.

Decades after World War II had ended, Japanese soldiers were being discovered on remote islands still fighting for their country. Some had not received word that the war was over; others simply refused to surrender. Victory in the Pacific was declared in 1945, and the last soldier discovered still holding out was in 1974 (*Time*, January 13, 1975). Our enemy operates much the same way—refusing to surrender even though his defeat has been accomplished and our ultimate victory assured. It does not come without battle, though. As surely as those aging soldiers were still holding out for victory, the Adversary and his minions launch assaults against us continually.

The intercessor, then, intersects the issue at hand with the triumph of the cross. We stand before the Father praying for those who are at the crossroads, interceding for the turning of people to a new way of life. It is wrapped up in the words: *Thy Kingdom come, Thy will be done on earth as it is in heaven.* That does not mean that we simply throw our hands in the air and say, "Well, Lord, Your will be done." As a matter of fact, the only two places in Scripture where the phrase *Your will be done* is used are in Jesus teaching us to pray and in His prayer to the Father regarding the cross. His will has been done! Redemption has been accomplished, and now we must follow His command and example to pray.

When we do, we are asking for the entry of Jesus' Kingdom rule into that situation. We are asking for God's original intention for that person or that circumstance to come to fruition. We are contending for the rout of the enemy who would still seek to make some believe that he has power. We are exercising the privilege of intersecting situations with the promised power of the cross.

Intervention

Intervention has to do with stepping in. For example, two sides are fighting and someone steps in, or intervenes, to bring peace. Intervention is that aspect of intercession where a person recognizes he or she has been given the right through Jesus Christ to invade a tough situation. We are given the privilege of moving into that situation in prayer, recognizing that someone needs to *step in* on behalf of the Kingdom. Jesus said, "All authority has been given to Me in heaven and on earth. Go therefore . . ." (Matthew 28:18–19). In other words, He is sending us backed by His authority. Wherever you go, the authority of the Kingdom will travel with you. "Make disciples . . . baptize . . . teach," He commanded; but as we saw in Jesus' ministry, it has to first be undergirded by prayer.

Let me give an example. You happen to hear that someone in your family, your neighborhood or your job is in a marriage that is disintegrating. You know the heartache that can emanate from that in children, couples, extended family. Homes are torn apart, finances decimated, trust betrayed, personal histories rewritten. You know that God never wants marriages to break apart. In fact His word says that "He hates divorce" (see Malachi 2:16) because of the destruction it causes in human hearts. Sometimes that seems impossible to imagine, but even in the middle of the worst kind of human error, chaos and confusion, God is capable of transforming any situation. Nothing shall be called impossible with God (see Luke 1:37). He is capable of redeeming anything! In fact, recently a woman came to our women's ministries director and said, "I stayed in my marriage only because you told me that God could fix anything. That was four years ago . . . and He's done it! He has fixed my marriage!"

Nothing shall be called impossible with God.

Now, because we have been given the choice of partnership with the Father, someone could also say, "It's too bad about John and Jane's marriage. I feel bad about that." They could simply leave it at the emotional level of empathy. John and Jane may even feel supported by empathetic friends. But empathy alone does little to elicit change in the situation. A person who knows his or her privilege in prayer hears the report, feels the "nudge" of the Holy Spirit and begins to respond. In intercession we can not only deal with the weaknesses of two people, but also challenge the heinous work of hell. There is a spirit of division at work when marriages come apart, so we can take a stance in prayer to push back the boundary that evil spirit has staked out, and begin to intercede as the Holy Spirit directs.

Another example is praying beyond those you know or praying for a nation. It is no more difficult to pray for a nation than it is to pray for two people you know. It is the same principle. You see something on the news and it tears your heart to see the suffering of people around the globe. Is it just the milk of human kindness? As sons and daughters of God, we have to decide what we believe is going on here, and again, we have a choice. We can just "feel bad" or we can pray. You see the account of an earthquake or flood, riots or economic upheaval. In prayer, you step in—intervene—between that spirit of chaos and the thousands of people for whom Christ died. You step in believing that what is taking place can be changed by the power of God, and His life can begin to flow into the situation. You choose to accept the privileged role you have as an intercessor.

Interception

The third word, *interception*, is what you see in an athletic competition, like football. The quarterback steps back and hurls a pass downfield to his receiver. Suddenly, in a flash, a backfield defender crosses in front of the intended receiver, seizes the ball and begins to work his way upfield—in the opposite direction.

What has happened is not only an interception, but *a complete reversal* in direction. An action that was intended to help defeat one team has turned into a victory for the other. This is not new for our Adversary, the devil. He thought he had won at the cross; but the cross was a complete reversal of what he expected.

The apostle Paul writes, "But we speak the wisdom of God in a mystery, the hidden wisdom which God ordained before the ages for our glory, which none of the rulers of this age knew; for had they known, they would not have crucified the Lord of glory" (1 Corinthians 2:7–8).

As surely as the cross stopped and reversed the activity of the Adversary, so does intercession. Through the power of the cross, the blood of our Savior and the name above every name, Jesus, we step in as ambassadors of the King and in His authority of the Kingdom overrule the situation.

The place of the intercessor, then, in perceiving himself or herself as a person who has large potential in prayer and ministry is fundamental to what the Church is to be. This is the reason that the Church in Antioch, having been well taught, could receive the Lord's word that He was going to change the world around them and through them (see Acts 13:1–3). They recognized that this change would involve three things:

1. People who worshiped—"as they ministered to the Lord"
2. People who interceded—"fasted and prayed"
3. People who obeyed the commission—willing to go wherever the Holy Spirit directed them

Make no mistake, such people make history. In the case of Antioch, it is fully verifiable that the spirit of worship, prayer life and obedience of the Lord's people in that church in Syria nearly two thousand years ago literally set the westward flow of the Gospel. The transforming power of the Spirit of God flows through praying people like us—beginning with Paul and Barnabas, and continuing to this day—and has brought the Church to this hour, approaching the climax of history.

So take your place. Let's tune to the voice of the Holy Spirit as He whispers, *I have drawn you to the Savior's life and grace, but now I want to shape you into His likeness as instruments of redemption.* We have seen in these last two chapters that intercession is the basic pattern for that to take place. As we receive and apply our understanding, be bold to believe! Such intercession in matters of individual and even worldwide scope will touch heaven and change earth as our prayer pierces the bonds of darkness with lightning-bolt accuracy and power.

6

IT'S ONLY BY THE BLOOD

To Him who loved us and washed us from our sins
in His own blood, and has made us kings and priests
to His God and Father, to Him be glory
and dominion forever and ever.

REVELATION 1:5–6

Whether people are familiar with the Old Testament or not, most are familiar with the story of Israel's Passover because of the movie classic *The Ten Commandments*. For decades it has continued to be given a place on television networks in the spring of the year as Easter and the Jewish Passover draw near. It presents liberation from slavery and the exodus from Egypt, replete with breathtaking scenes of the Red Sea opening before God's people and the vivid encounters between God and Moses. But this account in Scripture carries much more with it than just a moviemaking spectacular.

With this pivotal event in history, the Word of God sets forward an awe-inspiring demonstration of God's power and path to liberating not only people as individuals and families, but even a nation! The process of that deliverance unfolded as God sent a series of plagues on the land of Egypt. Each represented a confrontation with *both* Pharaoh's resistance and the demonic gods that the people of Egypt worshiped. Each plague demonstrated the Sovereign God's—our Father's—power to break the back of the real but limited power of the darkness of evil. Moses' continued confrontation of Pharaoh, and then his recurrent appeal to God to break through, is a study in spiritual warfare. But the greatest lesson in the epic struggle recorded in Exodus 5–13 is the message of redemption's source of ultimate power—the blood of the Lamb. As Pharaoh continued to refuse the release of God's people from slavery into freedom, each plague revealed God's greater power, but the last set forth the message of the fountainhead of all salvation and victory.

The Passover, as it was instituted here, gives us the underlying concepts necessary to understand all that God was ultimately to accomplish at the cross of Jesus Christ. The Passover provided the final judgment against Egypt, the world power of that era, prefiguring the power of the cross to defeat the dark powers that rule our world. What determined if a home came under judgment was the mark of the blood of the lamb on the doorposts. "The blood shall be a sign" (Exodus 12:13) provided protection for all who would come within its shelter and find freedom from certain destruction. The Passover is also a focal point for understanding the power of blood as it is used throughout Scripture in the redemptive process. All sacrifice in the Old Testament system is founded on the principle that it is through the offering of the blood of sacrifice that we receive great deliverance, great protection and a great God-provided future. This central tenet of the old covenant—freedom from sin and spiritual death through the blood of a lamb—is a mighty forecasting picture that was fulfilled in the Person of Jesus, the Lamb of God, at the cross.

In the case of the Passover, a witness was also provided—a reminder to current and future generations of the mighty workings of the Lord. In fact, to this day, the traditional Passover celebration will include the question, "Why is this night different from any other?" As believers in Jesus Christ, we can surely ask similar questions: "Why was this Man different? Why is this blood different? Why was His offering different?" Because it secured life for us; it secured freedom for us; it secured forgiveness for us. And it still does that today.

When we speak of the blood of Christ we are dealing with life. We are referring to what Scripture calls "precious" (see 1 Peter 1:19), and precious for a reason. As surely as the Passover lamb secured deliverance for Israel, Jesus' blood paid the inestimable price of liberty from the bondage of human sin, human failure and hellish spiritual torment. The blood of Jesus is so foundational to the universal order of things that the Bible refers to Jesus as the Lamb slain from the foundation of the earth (see Revelation 13:8).

Jesus had not even begun His ministry when John the Baptist announced the advent of the Messiah. When Jesus appeared at the waters of baptism, John stopped his preaching, looked at Him and said, "Behold! The Lamb of God who takes away the sin of the world!" (John 1:29). There was not one person listening to that declaration who would not have understood the implications of those words, but it would prove difficult for the "religious" ones to come to terms with the idea that Messiah, the King, was also the Lamb. Over centuries, the hope of a Messiah, which had first been prophesied as the one who would bruise the head of the serpent (see Genesis 3:15), had diluted to an expectation of political overthrow of hostile forces and the reinstituting of the Davidic kingdom. These things would all happen, but not in the way Israel had come to expect! The victory would be won—not through force, but through sacrifice. John was raising a signal not only to his hearers but to all of history.

When we talk about the subject of blood, most Western sensibilities cringe a bit. Blood is not something we encounter every day; and, in fact, depending on the person, we can become squeamish over a paper cut! But this was an agricultural society; the slaughter of animals for food, and the attendant bloodiness, was a daily occurrence in that culture. My wife, Anna, grew up in a rural environment. One of her chores as a child occasionally involved killing a chicken for dinner! It is hard for me to imagine that! It is hard for Anna to imagine now, too! That note is not to minimize the issue we are dealing with here, but simply to point out that the concept of the Lamb of God did not cause issue for Israel because of "blood"; it caused issue because their expectation was for a King. Still, they likewise knew from the Law—and they knew from daily life—*that life was in the blood* (see Leviticus 17:14), both spiritual and physical life.

LIFE IS IN THE BLOOD

In the Old Testament, when the food laws were being listed for the people, one of the principal laws was the forbidding of the eating of blood, because "the life is in the blood." We logically know that simply by the fact that someone can "bleed to death." Without blood, we cease to live. When it came to the Old Testament sacrifices, the concept held true, because an animal was now "bleeding to death" for your sin. The blood of that sacrifice covered the sin of the person offering the sacrifice. Of course, we know that those sacrifices were not permanent, but awaiting God's ultimate gift of the final sacrifice, Jesus. Hebrews 10:5 says, "For it is not possible that the blood of bulls and goats could take away sins. Therefore, when He [Jesus] came into the world, He said: 'Sacrifice and offering You did not desire, but a body You have prepared for Me.' " Jesus came to provide for us what we could not provide for ourselves. He shed His blood for us—as a covering, as a protection from sin and death, as a cleansing for sin and provision of forgiveness: There is life in His blood!

As we have addressed the issue of prayer, we have seen that any prayer power or partnership with the Father that we have has all been secured for us and released to us through the gift of the cross. But I would like to take a moment here to look specifically at Jesus' sacrifice, *what* it has provided for us and *how* it impacts our ability to penetrate the darkness through prayer.

As a child I was raised in church, and I would often hear people discuss the need to pray for difficult situations with the words, "We need to plead the blood." No one explained it to me, but I sensed even as a youngster that this was a right and wise thing to do. Yet, because I was a child, I attributed an incorrect definition to the word *plead*, and turned it, in my mind, into a sort of begging exercise. I was "pleading" with God. It was as though I had to beg God to do something nice: "Oh, please do this" or "Please don't do that. Oh, God! Oh, God! I just plead the blood!"

The longer I grew in the Lord, however, the more I realized that He has not called us to come begging before Him. Pagan deities require that: We see that in the books of the Kings when Elijah challenged the prophets of Baal (see 1 Kings 18). Those misguided priests were shedding *their own blood* in an effort to get their god to act in their behalf. No. God does not require begging from us; but He does want us to learn—and to access—the power of His sacrifice. I came to learn that just as Israel came "under the blood" at Passover, we, as believers in Jesus Christ and His sacrifice, can come "under" that protective covering. When we pray something like "Father God, we come under the blood of Jesus" or "Lord, please cover this matter with the blood of Jesus," a *spiritual dynamic* is operating. It is the dynamic of life.

In *The Chronicles of Narnia*, C. S. Lewis sought to explain some of these very deep theological concepts in a way that a child could grasp. In the story *The Lion, the Witch and the Wardrobe*, there are four main characters—brothers and sisters—who have stumbled into another world, Narnia. One of the brothers, Edmund, betrays the others to the enemy. The enemy—the White Witch—intends to kill the betrayer; but in order to save him and keep the family together, Aslan (who is a picture of Jesus Christ) offers himself in place of Edmund. Aslan will die in the place of the betrayer. The Witch, believing that she has found a way to eliminate her opponent, agrees, and kills Aslan.

Lewis writes brilliantly about Aslan's resurrection. Aslan explains that "when a willing victim who had committed no treachery was killed in a traitor's stead . . . death itself would start working backwards."

Backwards? Yes. Death working backwards is life! The power of the blood will always issue forth in life.

FOUR PROVISIONS IN THE BLOOD

We study the power of the blood because of its power to redeem us from the pull of sin and death, and to conquer the darkness with Kingdom light and life. Every believer in Christ should know how to appropriate the power of the blood of Jesus. Like the Passover, the blood has been applied to the doorways of our hearts. Now, just as surely as the blood provided for Israel then, it provides protection, deliverance and promise for our lives. It is the primary key for growing in the faith, boldness and breakthrough we long for. The Bible says,

> Therefore, brethren, having boldness to enter the Holiest by the blood of Jesus, by a new and living way which He consecrated for us, through the veil, that is, His flesh, and having a High Priest over the house of God, let us draw near with a true heart in full assurance of faith, having our hearts sprinkled from an evil conscience and our bodies washed with pure water.
>
> HEBREWS 10:19–22

Today as believers in Jesus Christ, we can appropriate four direct provisions by reason of the blood being shed for us. In understanding what has been provided for us, we learn what it means for us to access the power of what Jesus accomplished on the cross. When we "plead the precious blood of Jesus," we are claiming all that He has provided for us of protection from spiritual death, deliverance from the slavery of sin, a new beginning wherever hope has waned and a witness to a watching world. And in "pleading the blood," we are driving back the forces of darkness that seek to afflict our planet and inflict the ploys of the Adversary, because those hellish powers cannot stand before the power of the blood of Jesus Christ.

The Blood Provides Protection

Exodus 12:13 says, "Now the blood shall be a sign for you on the houses where you are. And when I see the blood, I will pass over you; and the plague shall not be on you to destroy you when I strike the land of Egypt."

A superficial look at this text might create doubt about God's character: Was He not being a little vindictive toward the Egyptians? Taking His actions in context, however, shows the incredible mercy of God: He provided Pharaoh with many opportunities to act appropriately. We see throughout the account of the plagues that some of the Egyptians even responded when Moses gave warning of upcoming plagues (see Exodus 9:20). While Pharaoh had his own reasons for refusing to respond, some of his people obviously listened and acted. Though it does not say in Scripture that any of the Egyptians specifically obeyed the warning and directions regarding this particular plague, there is no reason to think that there were not some who did. In fact, when Israel finally left Egypt, Scripture tells us that "a mixed multitude went up with them also" (Exodus 12:38). These were people who, though not part of Israel biologically, chose to align themselves with the people of God, based on what they had seen of God's mighty works. They accepted freedom and departed Egypt along with Israel. A careful study of Scripture reveals that throughout the Old Testament, whenever people sought to enter covenant with Israel's God, it was not denied them.

Thus, God was not acting vindictively; He was dealing redemptively. He was on the verge of bringing two million people out of slavery. Pharaoh should, at this point, have been on his knees before God thanking Him for his life and enthronement in Egypt. Instead he was still shaking his fist in God's face.

Before the night of visitation, the Lord directed the Israelites to take a lamb into each household for four days. Lambs were fairly common pets, and you can imagine that when the day came

for it to be slaughtered, the families—especially the children—would have become attached to the lambs. This act of obedience was laden with emotion because God was teaching a powerful lesson: Redemption has a high and painful price. The loss of these family pets was nothing compared to the heart of God who loved the world so much He gave His Son to die for it, but the death of innocent creatures made a point.

Imagine, if you will, the blood being drained from that lamb's small carcass and put into a basin, then, with the brush of the reeds, slapping the blood upon the side posts of their doors and on the lintels overhead. No one on that side of Calvary could have imagined that it was more than an umbrella over the door as it dripped down, but we see from this side a picture of the cross. The Lord was providing a way, not only for Israel's protection on that occasion, but also for the ultimate protection of all humankind: The judgment of death is on everyone who does not come under the protective cover of the blood of the cross of Jesus Christ. (See Romans 3:25; 5:9; Colossians 1:20; 2:14.)

The Blood Provides Deliverance

By the blood of the lamb, the people were given a means of deliverance. The blood that saved the Israelites was also the substance by which the yoke of Pharaoh's strength was broken.

After the angel of death struck down the firstborn of the Egyptians, God's covenant people were released from bondage literally overnight. There is no logical explanation why those uncovered by blood suffered so great a devastation. It was a miracle by every measure.

We see this same freedom from bondage alluded to again and again throughout the New Testament. Paul writes that we were "in bondage under the elements of the world" (Galatians

4:3), but like Israel in the wilderness, too many default to "the weak and beggarly elements" that lead again to bondage (Galatians 4:9). However, Christ's blood gives complete freedom—to walk with God (see Romans 8:15), to walk free from sin (see Galatians 5:1), to walk in liberty (see Luke 4:18). As Colossians 1:13–14 states: "He has delivered us from the power of darkness and conveyed us into the kingdom of the Son of His love, in whom we have redemption through His blood, the forgiveness of sins." Deliverance is ours! Freedom is ours! And it is all through the blood.

The Blood Provides a New Beginning

The Lord made the night of Passover an established beginning point: "This month shall be your beginning of months; it shall be the first month of the year to you" (Exodus 12:2). What happens through the blood opens the door of a new day!

Right now, you may be at what seems to be the end of your own hope and strength. You may be overwhelmed with financial burdens. Relationships around you may be crumbling—and you don't know what to do. Work or school or weariness or depression may be summoning all of your strength—and you don't see a light at the end of the tunnel. But through the power of the blood the promise comes to you, just as it came to Israel so long ago: "This will be the beginning of days to you." Through Jesus and His reconciling work for us at the cross, Scripture tells us that "if anyone is in Christ, he is a new creation; old things have passed away; behold, all things have become new" (2 Corinthians 5:17). Not only has He made us new, not only is today "the beginning of days to you," but through His cross we have a future and a hope for tomorrow (see Titus 3:7). "He who has begun a good work in you will complete it" (Philippians 1:6)!

The Blood Provides a Witness

As the blood was put over each door it gave testimony to the fact that here was a place of safety for anybody who wanted to come in. It gave testimony to where Israel was putting her belief and faith and trust. Can you imagine the bold stand these people had to take? They were being watched! They were not only slaves, but now they were making a belief statement. As noted above, some of the Egyptians at least believed enough that they were taking action on Moses' warnings. Still, the whole sacrifice ceremony and accompanying actions must have mystified the observers.

I sometimes wonder how much our homes give witness to the covering of the blood. When people come to your house or mine do they find anything different? Is the mood or atmosphere different from that of the world? I am not talking about religious pictures or plaques that "preach" from the various walls, but rather something that people can sense of the Spirit of the living God because the blood of Jesus covers our households. Is the atmosphere of heaven evident in your home without your even having to say a word? This invitation to come in out of the path of death should be just as true of our households as it was of the Israelites' homes.

The Israelites would surely have heard some mocking, even as the world today has no more value than Pharaoh had for the things that fill God's people with hope. But we are not of this world (see John 18:36). We are not peddling in the realm of superstition; we are functioning in the realm of the supernatural. God's people had received a realm of divine power that had insulated them from the forces of darkness and death in the land.

I guarantee that the morning after the Passover no sounds of mocking were heard. The stunned Egyptians would have been engulfed in grief and mourning, suddenly brought face-to-face with the results of their choice of unbelief. It will be the same in the end times—the times in which we live. At Jesus' coming, there will be those who can only lament the fact that it is now too late. Brothers! Sisters! *We must make our homes a testimony to all that Jesus has provided for us.* Everything is at stake for the world around us, for those we love, for those who have no other witness than how they see us live.

Our partaking of Communion (or the Eucharist or the Lord's table—however your tradition terms our remembrance of the Lord's death until He comes) is another way that we give witness to the power of the blood and what Jesus' cross accomplishes in our lives. First Corinthians 11:26–32 tells us that at the Lord's table, we are to examine ourselves so that we can receive healing and forgiveness, and we are to give testimony. "They overcame him [the Adversary] by the blood of the Lamb and by the word of their testimony, and they did not love their lives to the death" (Revelation 12:11). Every time you and I come to the Lord's table, we are celebrating in Jesus Christ, the Lamb of God, the same thing that the Passover lamb provided. It is the power of the blood that protects, that delivers, that opens a new day and that becomes a witness and an invitation to a watching world.

THE LEGAL GROUNDS

Now, we need to understand how all of this comes together, because God does not just arbitrarily do random acts, or display His power for the sake of simply showing His power. There is reason and intention behind the things that God does. His laws apply universally, and while He can supersede them, He chooses to act within them. He set them in place for a reason.

Thus, for Him to provide a way for humankind to be forgiven and come again into fellowship with Him, a just retribution for sin had to be satisfied: The sentence pronounced against us had to be met. The ticket had to be paid; the debt made good; the judgment against us fulfilled. God could not allow imperfect, blemished sinners into His presence; not because He is a snob, but because His holiness constitutes a "completeness" that would disintegrate all that is unholy. On our own, we would not be able to survive in His presence. A way had to be made, and that was done through the shed blood of Jesus Christ—whose blood legally covers our unholiness.

Once accepted, the power of the blood grants authority! Just as we saw at Passover, there were far-reaching effects in the lives of the people, based on the power of the blood and what it accomplished. Pleading the blood of Jesus is a heaven-given resource that grants us license to confront the darkness and to challenge and overthrow the works of hell, because the blood authorizes our extending its legal claim to expel evil. "Claiming the blood" is not a cry of desperation; it is a legal term available in the same sense as an attorney in court makes a "plea" on legal grounds, based upon a body of evidence.

When you and I come before the court of heaven in prayer, and "plead the blood," we are accessing that which is proven to neutralize the power of sin, the power of affliction, the power of death and the power of hell. Remember: In *every* circumstance we face in life we now have the legal right, through the blood of Jesus Christ, to enter a plea and to lay claim to the evidence— His slain body, His shed blood at the cross, His resurrection, His allocating His assigned authority to us as "partakers in the firm." The evidence on our behalf is due to what He accomplished at the cross. We have nothing of our own. It is to that legal right I make my plea when I plead the blood of Jesus. His blood purchased my salvation, and now, whether I face demonic, physical or personal attack, condemnation or the temptation to sin, I can lay personal claim to that same plea.

And what is my plea? That the defendant is not guilty. The defendant cannot be bound. Why? Because of the evidence of the blood reverifying the fact that my plea is just and appropriate. It verifies the fact that God's legal requirements for justice have been met and satisfied (see Romans 3:24–26).

The evil principalities and powers were marshalling their troops when they duped mankind into taking the Creator-Redeemer and killing Him on a cross in Jerusalem. The apparent victory of evil was no victory at all. The act of slaying the Lamb would rebound upon them, for in the mightiness of Jesus' resurrection He broke the power of evil forever. First Corinthians 2:7–8 says, "We speak the wisdom of God in a mystery, the hidden wisdom which God ordained before the ages for our glory, which none of the rulers of this age knew; for *had they known, they would not have crucified the Lord of glory.*" Satan thought he had won the day, but what was accomplished at the cross became his downfall. The victory was accomplished there, once and for all!

There is now, in fact, no circumstance in life in which the blood of Jesus is not key to God's releasing, protecting, delivering power, whether it is removing the potential of confusion, overcoming the impact of rebellion, breaking the torment of fear or healing the shame of the past. When we enter our plea, we are to do so on the basis of the evidence—the blood of Jesus Christ—and through it, all evil has been broken in its power, all sin neutralized, the power of death overwhelmed and every human need paid for once and for all. Whatever difficulty you face, stand firm and lay hold of the victory at hand when you plead the blood of Jesus.

SAFE UNDER THE BLOOD

Years ago, Anna and I were walking downtown through Colombo, Sri Lanka—that little island nation down at the toe of India. As we walked along the street we saw possibly every kind of human deformity as well as those things that characterize the superstitions so predominant in that part of the world. We were not feeling either judgmental or frightened, but we were deeply aware of the visible evidence of the entrenchment of evil. Because of that, we were praying quietly as we walked, "Lord Jesus, cover us with the blood as we walk along here." We were not speaking those words because we were afraid of being bitten by a snake being "charmed" nearby or of being attacked by the beggars on the street. We were simply moving in the wisdom and understanding that there is a covering—an encapsulating protection—through the blood of Jesus, and that we can lay hold of it.

As we were strolling along, we went into one shop that did not look much different from the others. But as soon as we entered I felt something almost like crackling on the back of my neck. I turned to Anna and asked, "Does this place feel funny to you?"

She said, "Yes, it does."

Looking around we did not see anything that would cause concern, but we decided to leave. Then on the way out we saw it: One whole wall was filled with every kind of resource for evil—everything from Satanic symbols to more minor expressions of the occult, such as incense and crystals.

Some people might say, "Well, those are just 'things,' artifacts people who are only dealing in superstition use." But listen: "Artifacts" acquire a sinister presence when people worship them. When people who embrace them have dedicated them sincerely and wholeheartedly to the worship of dark powers, they have empowered them by the fact they welcome demons. The Bible teaches there are demons that operate behind them, as the apostle Paul writes, "What am I saying then? That an idol is anything, or what is offered to idols is anything? Rather, that the things which the Gentiles sacrifice they sacrifice to demons" (1 Corinthians 10:19–20). In Deuteronomy 32:17, we read that Israel "provoked [God] to jealousy with foreign gods; with abominations they provoked Him to anger. They sacrificed to demons, not to God, to gods they did not know" (see also 1 Corinthians 8:5).

What we could feel in that little store was a demonic stronghold, and sensing that, we again prayed as we walked, "Father God, we claim the power of the blood of Jesus. We take cover in His cross and victory." Yes, the blood of Jesus provides protection for us when we are in spiritual combat zones!

Again, we were not afraid, but we were discerning, knowing the limits of the Adversary. Though he cannot contain or hold us, he can make an effort—just as a cat could reach out and claw you, the Adversary might atempt to use a small contact like that to disturb your mind at that moment, or even to sow something that you would feel the residue of later on. The Adversary has been defeated, but he will maintain or seek to gain a foothold wherever he can. Our discernment and constant warfare against him help to keep us protected from his ploys.

These are realities. The realm of the invisible—the supernatural existence of good and evil—is no less factual today than it was that night in Egypt long ago. The people of God embraced a realm of divine power that insulated them from death. They took the actions of faith and obedience to access an invisible realm. There are those who would trivialize the invisible. Yet, if we are honest, we have all had moments when we have felt this. For instance, you enter a room where you feel a hateful tension between two people. The force is real though invisible since tension is not a visible, tangible object. But it is often more then two people who cannot make up their differences. We may blame it on that, or we may better discern if an invisible adversary is seeking to divide them and destroy a relationship. "For we do not wrestle against flesh and blood, but against principalities, against powers, against the rulers of the darkness of this age, against spiritual hosts of wickedness in the heavenly places" (Ephesians 6:12). This is the awareness with which we are called to live—a small example of a great possibility.

Let me conclude this chapter by giving you two illustrations that honor the power of the blood, not in superstition but in an awareness of its spiritual strength to penetrate the darkness and set prisoners free.

POWER OVER EFFECTS OF SIN

Years ago I spoke at a conference, and afterward was praying with some of the young people. A fourteen-year-old girl asked for prayer to receive the baptism with the Holy Spirit, but just could not seem to break through. She loved Jesus, but her spiritual language had not been released to her. As we talked, she said, "My mind is so preoccupied, and I have nightmares all the time."

As we continued to talk and her story unfolded, I learned that she had recently gone to a rock concert against both the wishes of her parents and her own inner sense as a Christian. While there she had bought a poster, brought it home and hung it in her room. Her parents had asked her to take it down, but she was insistent in her rebellion. As we talked further, we discovered that the nightmares had begun that very night.

I explained to her what is no secret—that some in that industry admit how sometimes demonic powers are invited by musicians—literally worshiping or invoking the satanic realm of evil in exchange for worldly success.

As this young lady came to terms with her rebellion and the place it had given to the enemy, we prayed together and brought the situation under the blood of Jesus. I explained to her the power of the blood not only to make way for forgiveness for her rebellion but also to break the power that tormented her mind.

I gave her some instruction, and she decided to make a phone call to her mother. "Pastor Jack Hayford is praying with me here," she said. "Mom, will you take that poster off my wall and go burn it right now? And Pastor Jack said that when you take down each tack, say, 'I'm doing this in the name of and under the blood of Jesus Christ, the Son of God.' " Her mother was a committed believer and understood completely what was taking place. She burned the poster and pled the covering of the precious blood of Jesus.

The next day, not only was this girl baptized with the Holy Spirit, but at breakfast she came over to my table and told me, "I didn't have any nightmares last night!" I have little doubt that she never had any more on that order because she had broken through the darkness gripping her by pleading the power of the blood.

WASHED CLEAN

A young woman I will call Molly came to my office. She had a lesbian background and only months before had come to Christ at our church. When Molly came to my office that day her expression was very, very heavy.

"Pastor Jack," she began, "I know God has forgiven me of my past sin, but the shame of it stays on my mind. I can't escape the recollection of the things I allowed to be done with my body. And there are times that I feel the physical impact of that shame—as though the unnaturalness has polluted me." She paused and added, "I just came to ask you what I can do because I know I am saved, I know I am forgiven."

As we talked, I turned the conversation to the power of the blood of Jesus. I read from Hebrews 10:19–23, which says this (emphasis added):

> Therefore, brethren, having boldness to enter the Holiest by the blood of Jesus, by a new and living way which He consecrated for us, through the veil, that is, His flesh, and having a High Priest over the house of God, let us draw near with a true heart in full assurance of faith, *having our hearts sprinkled from an evil conscience and our bodies washed with pure water*. Let us hold fast the confession of our hope without wavering, for He who promised is faithful.

The Lord promises that through His cross, He will wash our bodies with pure water by reason of the power of the blood. He not only washes us, but frees us from even the conscience of sin. The Lord impressed an idea upon me, and I shared it with Molly.

While she was seated across from my desk I said, "Molly, I want you to imagine a basin here. I want you to imagine it full of the blood of Jesus because of the power of what He did at the cross. Now I am not talking about people who tear their own flesh in rituals to try to earn God's favor. I am talking about what Jesus did through His blood once and for all. That power is on reserve for us." And then I described a prophetic action for her to take.

Never take a prophetic action as a superstitious move; but neither should you hesitate to take one if you feel that is what the

Lord is telling you to do. Scripture is filled with God commanding His people to take prophetic action to signify what He is about to do; for example, as at the Passover. So I explained these things to Molly, and then continued.

"Molly," I said, "the Bible says that He washes our bodies with pure water because of what He accomplished through His blood. Now, I'm not initiating a ritual here, but an action to help connect with how real and complete what Jesus did for us is, seeing the cleansing blood in this imagined basin. I'm going to leave you here—just you and Jesus. I want you, first, to lock the door. Then I want you to prayerfully act out "washing your hands in the blood of Jesus." As you offer to Him all the things your hands have ever done, say this: 'I plead the cleansing of the blood and I remove those things from my conscience.' Then as the Lord leads you, I want you to offer every part of your body that you feel has ever been tainted or stained by the shame of sin. Indeed, imagine you are bathing your body in the cleansing blood of Jesus."

After I finished explaining this to her I left the room. About ten minutes later I came back and, as we had agreed, I knocked on the door. When she opened it her face was aglow, washed with tears. With a smile she attested to the power of the blood of Jesus. The Lord had washed away not only the restraining power of sin but the shame of it, the shame that continually accused and condemned her. Just as Molly learned, let us learn that what Jesus did on the cross not only provides forgiveness before the Father, but can cleanse us through and through—spirit, soul and body.

These testimonies are not given to try to "formulize" God. In fact, I am not recommending that you take these examples as a formula for anything. Rather, I would encourage you to ask the Lord how He wants you to apply the blood of Jesus to the doors of your life. But I urge you: See, as with the Passover, the power of Jesus' sacrifice for us. See, in the testimonies above, that there is no circumstance in your life for which the blood is not the key to the releasing power, to the protecting power, to the overcoming power against only darkness trying to hold you.

Scripture tells us that the delivering power of Jesus' sacrifice will be sung of forever. Would you join me in heaven's song of praise for Jesus' sacrifice right now? "You were slain, and have redeemed us to God by Your blood. . . . Worthy is the Lamb who was slain to receive power and riches and wisdom, and strength and honor and glory and blessing!" (Revelation 5:9, 12).

7

A BINDING CONTRACT

I will give you the keys of the kingdom of heaven,
and whatever you bind on earth will be bound in heaven,
and whatever you loose on earth will be loosed in heaven.

MATTHEW 16:18–19

Caesarea Philippi is one of the most beautiful places in northern Israel. It is a place of refreshing—green and peaceful. It is where the headwaters of the Jordan pour forth from beneath a gargantuan layer of solid rock. At the time of Christ, this location was also one of pagan worship. An alternative name for it is Banias, derived from the idol-god Pan, and there is evidence that idols to multiple gods and goddesses were erected at this site.

This is the place Jesus chose to ask His disciples, "Who do you say that I am?" (Matthew 16:15) . . .

- *at the place* where the water source for the whole nation pours forth . . .
- *at the place* where His divinity is contrasted with the world's incessant search for spiritual reality . . .

- *at the place* where, when Jesus said, "On this rock I will build My church" (verse 18), they had a vivid example, right before their eyes, of what He was talking about—rock-solid, unchanging, with rivers of living water pouring from it.

It is in *this* place that Jesus not only confirms His own divinity—as the Messiah, as God become flesh, and as the Redeemer—to come, to suffer, to die and be resurrected, but also proclaims these defining issues in the midst of a confusing human milieu—characterizing the emptiness, darkness and lostness of humanity. There in the ruin of our real world, He describes His strategy to "build My church" as a people who penetrate the spiritual darkness that surrounds all of humankind.

When Jesus came into the region of Caesarea Philippi, He asked His disciples, saying, "Who do men say that I, the Son of Man, am?" So they said, "Some say John the Baptist, some Elijah, and others Jeremiah or one of the prophets." He said to them, "But who do you say that I am?" Simon Peter answered and said, "You are the Christ, the Son of the living God." Jesus answered and said to him, "Blessed are you, Simon Bar-Jonah, for flesh and blood has not revealed this to you, but My Father who is in heaven. And I also say to you that you are Peter, and on this rock I will build My church, and the gates of Hades shall not prevail against it. And I will give you the keys of the kingdom of heaven, and whatever you bind on earth will be bound in heaven, and whatever you loose on earth will be loosed in heaven." Then He commanded His disciples that they should tell no one that He was Jesus the Christ. From that time Jesus began to show to His disciples that He must go to Jerusalem, and suffer many things from the elders and chief priests and scribes, and be killed, and be raised the third day.

MATTHEW 16:13–21

It is worth rereading this pivotal passage, for it is there Jesus promises to give the "keys of the kingdom of heaven" to those who know who He truly is; and it is also there He introduces the dual concepts of "binding" and "loosing." In doing so, Jesus joined His endowment of His people with keys of the Kingdom to their need to be capacitated to move in dimensions of prayer and spiritual ministry to exercise His delegated authority to "bind" or "loose." This potential, designed as His foremost means to enable *applied* prayer in distinct and demanding situations, calls for the shaping of a host of believers—alive in Christ and in partnership with Him. Jesus' call to discipleship is a call to those who will learn:

1. To pray that the "gates [strategies] of hell" should not prevail

2. To pray empowered prayer ("whatever you may bind/loose on earth") drawing heaven's overcoming power ("has already been bound/loosed in heaven") into the present moment

In the light of this text from Matthew 16 (above), it is helpful to join it to the Lord's Prayer (see Luke 11:1–4), which demonstrates how clearly, simply and powerfully Jesus connects *prayer* to His Church-building plans; to return people to their intended partnership between heaven and earth. In responding, we need to understand both the importance of prayer and the nature of the "tools"—that is, the strategies for prayer that God's Word presents. This pivotal text is best understood with a short lesson in the grammar of the New Testament. It will help us see how *prayer* and Jesus' accomplished *redemption* relate when we pray *"Your Kingdom come, Your will be done on earth as it is in heaven"* (Luke 11:4, in the light of Matthew 16:19).

Whatever you bind/loose on earth. Literally, both Greek verbs (bind/loose) in *tense* and *mood* indicate that the promise is *conditional*, requiring participative, appropriating prayer regarding specific situations on the earth-side of the partnership. The person praying *may* "bind" (that is, restrict or require according to God's revealed Word and will) or "loose" (that is, release or free the intended purpose of God's sovereign power). One limit to the believer's authority is God's wisdom in His answer and timing; but, amazingly, the primary limitation is this: *Will you, or I, or anyone else pray?* This is exactly what qualifies Jesus' teaching on binding and loosing: It is in the five words following "on earth." The target of prayer is the invoking of *God's* will—His *rule* from His Throne of love and power—awaiting prayer's call, "Father, let Your kingdom come 'on earth . . .

'. . . *as it is in heaven.*' "

The grammar is profound. A literal rendition of the verbs *shall be bound* and *shall be loosed* into English is that each "shall *already have been* bound or loosed." The verb form in each case reflects action achieved in the past that now becomes effected in the present. The *past* action is a clear reference to *Jesus' consummate triumph through His cross,* for it is there He secured in heaven *all* release of redemption's future workings. His "It is finished" becomes functional where it is welcomed and applied—both on earth in the visible realm and in the heavenlies in the face of all dark powers of fleshly and satanic origin.

Thus, the composite statement Jesus is teaching establishes a scope of human participation with authority, endowed as a gift to be applied in prayer and ministry with humility before the

Sovereign God who has willed this and extended this privileged partnership through His Son. Thus, "all prayer" is called forth and becomes effective:

- *by reason of Jesus' perfect redemption* and release of all grace through His perfect work of salvation's price by His blood and death on the cross (see Colossians 2:13–15); and

- *when this partnership* (1) has been entered and exercised by anyone who knows, receives and confesses Christ as Lord and King, the Son of God and Savior (see Matthew 16:15–17), and (2) thereby is acknowledged by the Lord Jesus in the presence of the Father and before all angelic powers, whether faithful angels or Satan's fallen host (see Matthew 10:32; Luke 12:8); and

- *wherever stance in prayer is taken* against "the gates of hell" (that is, the counsels, strategies, devices of the Thief's and Liar's plots or personnel, however evident; the stance being sustained in contending faith that rests in Christ's cross and its ever-present penetrating power, inevitably overcoming the Adversary's relentless, age-long efforts to prevail).

We have looked at how this applies through our exercising of intercession, but now we turn to the concepts of binding and loosing, because they reveal two more kinds of prayer. First Timothy 2:1–4 presents a call to each of them, along with other prayer expressions:

> Therefore I exhort first of all that supplications, prayers, intercessions, and giving of thanks be made for all men, for kings and all who are in authority, that we may lead a quiet and peaceable life in all godliness and reverence. For this is good and acceptable in the sight of God our Savior, who

desires all men to be saved and to come to the knowledge of the truth.

In that verse, Paul writes of three types of prayer; and we would be remiss if we looked at that verse and supposed that he is simply stating various synonyms for *prayer*. Rather, he is revealing multiple aspects or features of prevailing prayer—and here, we will explore *supplication*.

Growing up in church, my perception of *supplication* became about the same as most believers: It was as though it suggested "a little more sincere or earnest form of prayer." I remember once thinking that through. I wondered, *Doesn't that suggest, then, that some praying is semi-sincere or maybe somewhat earnest, and then there is the* really *sincere prayer?* But it obviously was an almost laughable proposition: "First half-diligent prayers and then three quarters-diligent prayers, and occasionally (Hallelujah!) we finally apply a fully diligent prayer!"

Of course that is ridiculous; so I concluded that supplication must mean a lot more than simply an intensified form of prayer. Later, at study, I came to find that *supplication* is a specific kind of prayer—one that focuses the truth in Jesus' words regarding binding and loosing.

In fact, the word translated "supplication" traces back to the root word to *bind*. The word is *deesis* and simply means "a petition, prayer or request." But *deesis* has its root in the verb *deo*, which literally means "to bind, to knit, to tie or to wind." This is a remarkable connection when we consider that it is the same verb Jesus uses in Matthew 16:19—"Whatever you bind . . ."

It is likewise significant to note that this passage is in response to Peter's declaration that Jesus is the Christ; upon which pronouncement, Jesus immediately begins to teach that the development and construction of His Church will be the outflow—that essential understanding—of who He truly and fully is, as the God-Man incarnate, here to open the *Way* for humankind to know the *Truth* and to re-enter, be reborn and returned to the *Life* as God intended it from the beginning. So, with His eyes on that plan being advanced through His Church—"in miniature" in Peter, or an example of His plan for us all—Jesus' response to Peter's powerful declaration shows us His intention. Jesus' response to Peter's powerful declaration shows us His intention. He says, "You are Peter, and upon this rock" (that is, Peter's declaration), "I will build My church." *Peter* means "a piece of rock or a small stone," whereas the phrase *upon this rock* uses the word for "a large or great rock"—a towering monolith, not unlike the renowned Gibraltar. Peter later writes compellingly about this concept—that all who believe are "living stones"— once inert, dead in sin, but now alive in Christ to be "built up [into] a spiritual house" (1 Peter 2:5), a habitation for God. Peter clearly understood his place as a believer and servant of the Savior, and emphasized what Jesus taught them and is always the case now: He is calling His people to partnership. Peter knew—*and so can we!*—that the victory is His and these above texts unite to verify how the release of the keys of the Kingdom are linked to the triumph of the cross.

Further, the primary ground of victory and authority as being in the cross is supported at this point; for it is at this moment Jesus begins to turn *toward* the cross. Upon Peter's declaration, Jesus *immediately* begins to reveal to His disciples that He will face death; and in the gospel record, His next steps begin His journey to Jerusalem (see Luke 9:51). He meant our understanding of who He is, and how and where the release of His authority to His Church would be secured was at Calvary. And it is always *there* "beneath the cross of Jesus" that His Church is released for ministry to advance in faith, prayer and victory. So it is thus we live today on the "it is finished" side of the cross—extending and applying His victory "on earth," as it was achieved on that day when His victory was accomplished "in heaven."

Now, through the power of the cross, we can do more than merely become indignant when we see the Adversary at work in our world and in the lives of those around us. If we move in prayer, "warring" in the *spiritual realm*, where the outcome will be decided, He has already established His Kingdom victory, and given His Church the keys to *now* unlock the chains that hold people captive. Jesus has directed us, according to the Word of God, to "bind and loose" in prayer.

What exactly is meant by "being bound or loosed"? The answer is broad because the works of darkness are multi-faceted. People or circumstances are "bound." Nations and rulers are "bound." But, so is the Adversary's intention for evil. He is totally given to steal, kill and destroy in the same way we often describe someone "bound to" or "certain to" do the wrong thing. The issue of where the resistance lies and all we are to confront with the spiritual authority that the Kingdom keys represent is explained in Jesus' words *the gates of hell shall not prevail.*

RISE IN PRAYER'S COUNTERATTACK

Having clearly established the place of the Church in relationship to Himself, Jesus describes the counterattack He is commissioning against the darkness. To understand the purpose of the Church, next listen to Jesus' declaration that *"the gates of hell will not be able to prevail"*—not be able to understand *the Church*. To clearly see the scope of these words, let me discuss with you the idea behind "the gates" terminology.

In ancient times, the gates of a city would have functioned much as city hall would today. Contracts were legalized at the city gates. Property transfers were processed. War counsels were held. In other words, the gates were the *power center* of the community, and the *courts* of the local government. When Jesus said that "the gates of hell will not be able to stand against it," we find that again, grammar supports our study. The verb form of *prevail* implies *ongoing action.* Jesus was in effect saying that the evil administration, the counsels, devices and the strategies of the Adversary's hellish works against humankind would *increasingly* be impacted and crumble under the assault of Jesus' Church as His people would walk in the power of the cross—applying the will of the Father here on earth.

So it is that in using the metaphor of "the gates of hell," Jesus has announced that He has given us keys to "penetrate" those gates! The figure of speech gives us understanding that the councils or actions obstructing the will of God as a barricade of ensconced rule or governance cannot stand! "The keys" are placed in our hands—yours, mine, God's people's—to unlock, to overthrow or to cast down the gates of hell. The rule of darkness must yield when obedience to apply faith in prayer against hellish resistance is exercised. As surely as Jesus said that He has come to proclaim liberty to the captives (see Luke 4:18), the keys that He puts into our hands authorize His people to open or close, to unlock or lock, to bind or to loose.

PUTTING BINDING INTO PRACTICE

When we studied the concept of intercession, we looked at the definition of "chance encounters." When we look at supplication, we see complementary contrast. Supplication in many respects involves a considerably methodical, persistent approach to prayer. Having noted how the root word of *supplication* means "to bind, to knit, to tie, to wind"—all involving methodical activity—lets look at four illustrations to see picturesque examples of how binding works to penetrate the darkness.

Binding Off

My mother was a quintessential example of the Proverbs 31 woman. She was committed to our family and home. She served the Lord and was involved in the church. She developed several home-based businesses; and despite all of her "outside" activities, the family never suffered. She brought creativity and ministry-purpose to everything she did. One of the ways she expressed her creativity was by knitting. I would like to use this rather homespun example to illustrate the first thing that is happening when we bind things in prayer.

If you have ever knitted, you know that if you slip the loops off the needles, the whole piece you are working on can come unraveled. To prevent this from happening when you are finished with your project, you have to bind off. *Binding off* is the knitting term for finishing off what you are working on in a stitch that secures, or ties up, the last row so that the piece does not come apart.

When you bind in prayer in this way, you are stopping the unraveling. We see this happen all around us. You see a marriage that is coming apart; you have a friend whose child is suddenly separating himself from the family in a way that is unhealthy. It leaves loose ends in the family that need to be brought back together—knitted back in, as it were. A deal at work is starting to fall apart; a business is about to come undone. Nations break agreements and the unraveling goes on. In supplication, we can bind off this unraveling in the Spirit and see the situation redeemed, restored and renewed.

Bind Up

When we use the term *bind up*, the most obvious picture that comes to mind is that of bandaging an injury. The prophet Ezekiel writes of God binding up the broken (see Ezekiel 34:16), and the psalmist says that He will bind up our wounds (see Psalm 147:3).

Years ago, a family in our congregation was facing a divorce. Divorce always comes at a cost, but this was one of the messiest I had ever encountered. In the midst of the confusion, I sought to reach out to the husband whose children were taken from him, whose life had turned upside down and whose emotional state had reached its breaking point.

I was rebuffed at every turn.

It turned into a very awkward situation of not even being allowed to try to minister. I went before the Lord asking Him what I should do. The man clearly needed help and support, but seemed to be withdrawing into dangerous isolation. As I prayed, I was completely unprepared for the graphic picture the Lord showed me of the man's heart—literally in shreds, cut to ribbons and covered with blood. The Lord whispered to me that sometimes a person is so wounded that even a loving touch hurts. There was nothing for me to do but pray—in this case, with supplication— with binding up. This man's heart was so wounded that he was incapable of understanding or bringing any degree of health to his marriage at the moment. He needed people who would begin to bind up his wounds in prayer. Eventually, he began to heal enough that he was able to accept the loving touch of one-on-one ministry. But where he started was with the need to simply have his wounds bound up. We do that with supplication.

In our world—on this worn and torn planet earth—there are certain things that will never change unless we take a stance against the Adversary and his devouring pursuit of humanity (see 1 Peter 5:8). Scripture tells us that the Adversary is a thief, a murderer and a destroyer (see John 10:10). There are those all around us who bear the wounding of his tooth-and-claw, fire-and-fury actions—but as we come in supplication to the Lord, a prevailing, patient prayer pursuit will see wounds bound up, loss recovered, death driven back and destruction's rubble removed as God's grace flows into the world of individuals, families, congregations, communities and nations—recovering and rebuilding the lives of multitudes.

There will be times we need to come in supplication for ourselves as well, binding the works of the Adversary in our own lives. For example, have you ever noticed how the Adversary will not quit even after we have come and confessed a failure or sin to the Lord? Satan is a master legalist, and though the Lord has forgiven us, Satan will launch a campaign against our minds, recounting every sin, taunting us with our pasts. That is why he is called "the accuser" (Revelation 12:10), and we can either live under his condemnation or take a firm and faith-filled position against him, raising the claim of the cross of Calvary, in Jesus' name, to bind up the accusation—that is, tie down, as a seaman stops something from flapping in the wind.

The result of supplication's binding prayer will be peace. The Hebrew concept of peace, wrapped up in the word *shalom*, encompassed not only an absence of confusion, but wholeness and health. When we bind up in the name of Jesus, health and peace begin to flow. The term *supplication* is used often throughout Scripture, but one of my favorite verses of applied supplication is Philippians 4:6–7:

> Be anxious for nothing, but in everything by prayer and supplication, with thanksgiving, let your requests be made

known to God; and the peace of God, which surpasses all understanding, will guard your hearts and minds through Christ Jesus.

That verse is a Kingdom key if you take it in hand!

You and I do not have to live under the weight of oppression in the world around us—disturbed, overwhelmed and weary. When Jesus said that His "yoke is easy and [His] burden is light" (Matthew 11:30), it is because of the very partnership into which He calls us. We are never alone, because there is Someone in the yoke next to us—Christ Jesus our Lord—and He bears the greater part of the burden. The Bible says that "in everything by prayer" we can bring our requests before the Father, present them with supplication, sustain our praiseful stance with thanksgiving and anticipate the Savior's certain triumph. The immediate benefit where simple faith is grown to participate in the reality of the truth we are studying is *peace*—peace beyond what we can imagine; peace that brings healing; peace as a result of binding up.

Bind Together

Writers, poets and hymn writers have taught all to sing this truth in relational terms: "Lord, bind us together in love." As surely as we stop unraveling by binding off, there are times that situations then need to be bound together—knitted unto an abiding union. This is depicted in Malachi's words when he describes the need for "the hearts of the fathers [to be turned] to the children, and the hearts of the children to their fathers" (Malachi 4:6). We live in a broken world that deals in misunderstanding and misinformation. Daily we are assaulted by the hellish bombardment of lies that seek to divide and destroy human relationships, churches and nations. Every day we encounter situations in the lives of people where the power of binding together could well be the beginning point of seeing a relationship put back together and hearts turned toward one another.

In Matthew 18:15–20, Jesus made a pointed comparison between disagreements and agreements, how, in both, there is a need for hearts to be bound together. He describes the process of resolving relational issues by involving other witnesses, "that by the mouth of two or three witnesses every word may be established." Even in confrontation, there was not to be the arbitrary one voice against another, but the agreement of two or three. Jesus then goes on to point out that "if two of you agree on earth concerning anything that they ask, it will be done for them by My Father in heaven. For where two or three are gathered together in My name, I am there in the midst of them." These two verses also reveal Jesus again affirming binding and loosing; here, He does this in reference to the common or often critical need for binding together of the hearts of people—neighbors, spouses, church members, rivals—resolving and healing relationships and in joining together in prayer. Either way, He calls us to bind our hearts together.

Another way we can bind together is to be aware of people who are alone. The psalmist wrote that the Lord "sets the solitary in families" (Psalm 68:6). So often people isolate themselves when they are lonely, hurt or afraid. Yet the Lord says that He wants to put them into families—families of friends, families within the Body of Christ, families of their own. The isolation to which many have retreated is due to broken relationships that need to be bound together. Other times, there are relationships that do not yet exist that need to be bound together; however, assisting or inviting people into small group fellowships or prayer groups sets an atmosphere where the healing of prayerful partnership and friendship will eventuate in faith that binds together.

One of the elders in our church had a unique burden to pray for marriages to take place in our congregation. He and his wife led one of our congregation's home groups; and often, because of the ages of their own children, they would have many unmarried men and women come to their home group who had accepted the Lord in their late twenties and thirties. Some had missed "the marriage window," some had cut off ungodly relationships when they had come to the Lord . . . yet these people longed for a life partner. This couple began to lay hands on those young people and ask the Lord to bring someone into each of their lives, binding hearts together, and establishing godly marriages, homes and families. And He started to do that! It is a classic case of seeing the Lord doing exactly what we mentioned above.

Of course that is not the only way things and people are bound together. You see the tension between business partners, broken friendships and family members disowning one another. A member of our congregation once described to me the impact of a death in her family. Her father had died, and she said, "I feel as if my life is a picture puzzle that used to be all put together and formed a beautiful picture. Suddenly someone has ripped a bunch of pieces out of it, and told me that now I have to make a complete picture without those pieces." Something needed to be put back together. In all of these situations, we can step in with binding prayers that short-circuit the plans of darkness to destroy people's lives.

Enforcing a Contract

Let's look at one more way that supplication's binding in prayer may be applied. First let's draw a picture to illustrate our point. Let's say you are planning to add a room onto your house. One day as the work gets underway you realize that the room is not quite as big as the blueprint you agreed to in the contract. You measure it off and, sure enough, it is two feet too short. You have paid for a 25-foot extension and it measures only 23 feet. The contractor is obligated to make corrections that fulfill his legal agreement. His contract is "binding"; it gives you a legal right to require the changes be made. It gives you a right, as we discussed in an earlier chapter, to "intercede into" the intended dimensions or boundaries of the project. Because of the presence of a contract, and the legal agreement that has been made, the contractor is now required by law to correct the situation. This is not something that you have to beg him for; it is inherent in the contract.

Supplication is not a posture of begging God to do something, any more than you should have to beg a contractor to do what he said he would do. So we are not begging God; but we are entering into negotiations to enforce His contract—the contract that has been purchased by the blood of Jesus. Jesus has contracted liberty and deliverance and healing for people, but the Adversary is seeking to shortchange them. Our Adversary, the devil, cannot survive wherever the contract of the cross is brought to bear. But—like our hypothetical contractor—if what he is doing remains unchallenged, the boundaries will always remain too small. In prayer, we are called to hold the Adversary to God's contract.

The early Church knew both the importance and practice of prayer by Jesus' own example. They had been taught to pray with the conviction that they were bringing God's will into circumstances, because they had seen Jesus do it. They were also well-taught in the Scriptures, and knew that the promises of God are given for our bold and believing application. The lessons of the Old Testament are not simply for academic study, but for prophetic application (see Romans 15:4; 1 Corinthians 10:6).

In Acts 4, the early Church was facing persecution; they were being told to stop preaching in the name of Jesus. So they gathered together in the Upper Room, and started praying Scripture. They stood on the eternal Word of God and began to apply God's "contract" as binding, through supplication. "Your Word says this, Lord. Your Word says that people would rise up against Your Christ, Your Messiah, and against Your people. It happened under Pilate and it's happening now. So now we pray, Lord, stretch forth Your hand toward Your disciples and cause there to be manifestation of Your glory. We ask for boldness to preach! We ask for miracles among the people."

When they were finished praying, Acts 4:31 says that the whole place was shaken. The word used for prayer here is *supplication*. It is not translated that way into English, but it is the word that is used—*deomai*. As they prayed, something was bound up: They were all refilled with the power of the Holy Spirit, and they went out and the power of God was seen wherever they went. They began laying death blows to the works of darkness and seeing the life of the living God flow.

When we exercise binding prayer, then, we are being called to (1) deal with situations that are unraveling, so that wholeness can be brought to bear upon that situation and "disintegration" halted. We step in by the authority of Jesus' cross, and (2) bind up wounds to see healing come to the brokenness; we are called to pray for the (3) bringing together of things and people that are fractured or separated; and we are called to (4) enforce the binding contract of the living God that was secured at the cross. The challenge for us, as we boldly step out in supplication, is to hear and discern what the will of the Lord is.

SEEKING GOD'S INTENTIONS

Walking in the authority of the Lord, bearing the keys of His Kingdom never gives us the right to predetermine what God wants to do. That is presumption of the first degree. It is not our job to go about making our own judgments in any situation. Let me put this another way: God is not obligated to answer prayers that are spoken without having entered into consultation with Him first.

I marvel at the number of people who have been led to think that God is obligated to do anything we say. We once stayed at someone's vacation home, and over the door they had hung a plaque that announced: "What I confess, I possess." Positive speech is not a matter of getting God busy because we learn to quote a verse as though it were a slogan. There are so many who think that they can reel off any kind of request that they want. They argue this way: "Doesn't the Bible say, 'Ask what you will'?" (see John 15:7). And . . . yes, it does. But coming before the Lord in humility and making my requests known to Him is certainly not the same thing as presuming that we can use Scripture to twist God's arm to get whatever we want. God is not offering us a wand to wave or a chant to mutter.

I was once told of a person who would write in the memo line of every tithe check what he expected the Lord to give him because he was paying his tithe. *A speedboat. A new house. A better job.* He was challenged by an elder in his congregation who questioned, "Do you think you can *buy* a blessing from God?" The leader went on to help him see the confusion that had been sown into the mind of this sincere but misguided man.

God does not owe us anything; yet He offers us everything. And it is all purely by grace. My observation is that when we allow ourselves to "decide what should happen here," we have put ourselves as the priority, rather than focusing on praying for the people around us. Then if things don't turn out the way we prayed, we wind up compelled to cast blame on the other individual. "You didn't have enough faith." Or "There must be sin in your life." This is not how God calls us to live. We are to move in response to Him, not the other way around.

Instead, supplication calls us, not to the presumption of deciding what we are going to bind in prayer, but to humbly come into conference with God, remembering again how deeply He longs to have us partner with Him: "Father, what is Your will in heaven that I may declare it on earth? Help me to discern this situation so that I may move on it in prayer power." He wants us to learn how to move in response to what He intends to do, and as the Holy Spirit helps us discover the Father's mind on the matter, we know we have the grounds for our authority for the prayer that is supplication.

Praying this way requires that we listen for His voice, and He can speak to us in many ways. Scripture talks about the Lord speaking through nature (see Psalm 19:1), speaking through one another (see 1 Thessalonians 5:11) and giving revelation through gifts of the Spirit (see 1 Corinthians 14:1–6). Yet in my years of serving Him, I have found that the way He speaks most often is through His Word. I believe there are basic reasons for that.

First, He speaks through His Word because it is the *revealed* and *written* revelation of God. "All Scripture is given by inspiration of God, and is profitable for doctrine, for reproof, for correction, for instruction in righteousness, that the man of God may be complete, thoroughly equipped for every good work" (2 Timothy 3:16–17). Second, Scripture is our plumb line—the measuring instrument by which *everything* gets evaluated. Just as a surveyor uses a plumb line to make sure that everything is measured accurately and with precision, so are we to relate to God's Word, the Bible. No matter what you think God may have "told" you, if it does not line up with Scripture, it wasn't Him. Period.

Dear brother, dear sister, as believers, if we want to live and learn to walk with the Lord and hear His voice, we must build and maintain such a walk as engages in studying His Word, and in prioritizing its authority. When He speaks to us, the plumb line to determine what we believe He is saying will give evidence of a parallel agreement: The Word will verify and confirm it.

When we are developing our understanding of prayer to integrate it into all of life, I am reminded of how I used to segment my prayer time. I was inclined to think that prayer constituted one side of my devotional time and reading the Bible another, until one day I came to see that God gave the Word and prayer to interface, entwine and enter into the same flow. We come into His presence and let Him teach us and speak to us and direct us; and then we begin to learn where we can function, what we are to do in responding to a particular situation, and how we are to pray with clarity, focus and confidence.

PREVAILING IN PRAYER

When we take up our Christ-given, ordained privilege of receiving and exercising the use of the keys of the Kingdom and begin binding on earth what the Lord has bound in heaven, we will prevail in prayer. That is why Jesus said that the gates of hell—the plans, counsels, purposes, designs and devices of darkness—will not prevail. And remember, *prevail* implies ongoing action, the methodical, consistent process of prayer that we noted earlier. It is a result of people who take a settled and permanent stance in prayer.

It is that stance that will withstand the encroaching works of hell and darkness—the "shadows" of death in our world that bring affliction, that hold families in despair, that reduce businesses to rubble, that bind up nations. It is into this darkness God is calling for people who are willing to take a stance—an ongoing stance—to penetrate the darkness and to prevail in Jesus' name, applying the triumph of His cross, which has secured victory in the heavenlies and which binding prayers welcome into specific need and circumstances on earth.

We are living in a world where the ongoing warfare continues. But Jesus Himself has declared His overcoming promise: "To him who overcomes I will grant to sit with Me on My throne, as I also overcame and sat down with My Father on His throne. 'He who has an ear, let him hear what the Spirit says to the churches' " (Revelation 3:21–22). The message is clear: *You* overcome doubt and welcome Christ's readiness to enter situations into *this* realm of earth's broken kingdom and hell's dark rule. As we do, He will *enter*. His overcoming victory will penetrate the scene. The darkness cannot withstand the King of Light and Life.

8

BREAKING LOOSE

*Stand fast therefore in the liberty by which Christ has made us
free, and do not be entangled again with a yoke of bondage.*

GALATIANS 5:1

When one of my granddaughters was about four years old, her
parents took her to the store to buy her some new shoes. They
were shocked when they measured her feet and discovered that
she needed shoes that were two whole sizes larger! Unknown to
them, their daughter just kept scrunching her feet smaller and
smaller, rather than telling them that her shoes were too tight. Her
accommodation of her discomfort was obviously unnecessary, but
her independent choice to keep "scrunching" was based on her
childlike supposition that she had to come up with a solution.
Of course, it wasn't a solution, and her folks immediately took
her to get new shoes.

How often do we do the same thing ourselves. Things—life,
circumstances, problems—feel constricting and unyielding, clos-
ing in around us. The relentlessness of the Adversary continually
squeezes the challenges of life around us, ties us in knots over

feelings about our weakness, taunts over the brokenness in our hearts or presses in with reminders of past sin. And how often do we live in the supposition that the "too tight" situation requires our treating it as though it is normal, when, to the contrary, God in Christ has provided everything we need to be released—loosed into our future?

Having pastored so many of God's kids over so many years, I feel something of a concerned affection for dear believers who endure some things that are not intended to test our endurance as, certainly, some things are. But in either case, there is one towering truth that rises over all. Victory is always the intended outcome. New life is intended to fully afford "new shoes" for the Father's children. At times their design may differ from what we would have picked, but in the end stepping into His Father-designer-shoes will always "set my feet [yours as well] in a wide place" (Psalm 31:8).

Having begun with so homey a story, let me proceed—inviting you to join me in elaborating the binding and loosing concept further. I believe Jesus wants to press it into the heart and soul of His whole Church—especially to confront any who would accept the terms of or believe that we are consigned to a theology of fate. Jesus said that He would give us the keys of the Kingdom of heaven, "and whatever you bind on earth will be bound in heaven, and whatever you loose on earth will be loosed in heaven" (Matthew 16:19). And yes, this gargantuan gift carries with it provisions and conditions in equal balance and we need to understand both. Having developed the key of binding, we will now look at another—the key of loosing.

IN HIS AUTHORITY

First, let us understand "authority."

Both of these keys—binding and loosing—can be grossly

misunderstood and unwisely or even superstitiously applied if we do not understand the meaning of these keys and the grounds for the authority in which Christ calls us to live and pray. Nothing that the Lord has released to us through His cross is to be treated like a "magic bullet" or a lucky rabbit's foot. There is a lesson in the Old Testament that tells of the superstitious attitude with which the Israelites regarded the Ark of the Covenant. (Read 1 Samuel 4:1–11 to see how it backfired on them.) Another case is in the New Testament when religious superstition motivated the effort to cast out a demon. The persons involved had no perspective on either the understanding of, or relationship with, Christ necessary for their attempted exorcism (see Acts 19:13–16). These illustrations are not said to intimidate anyone, but they are a reminder that all of the gifts of God released to us through the cross of His Son, Jesus, are to be treated with wisdom, humility and a balanced approach.

Over the years, I have encountered those whose idea of spiritual authority seems to be defined by zeal—by an expenditure of either physical or supposed spiritual energy, believing that binding and loosing are based on "getting the words right," or certain physical actions to exuberantly "show our authority."

There are times that the Lord gives us a "prophetic" sense of words to speak or action to take in ministering. But there are no formulas with God. We greatly mistake the meaning of walking in His authority by simply raising voices or becoming excitable. Ministry of any kind certainly does not require saying an *abracadabra* or learning a secret handshake or a formula. And we are not assigned to chase down demons. What we are called to do is to stand against dark powers in what has been provided for us through the cross—to address situations the Lord directs us to in Jesus' name, with the promptings the Holy Spirit gives us, just as Jesus said: "Most assuredly, I say to you, the Son can do nothing of Himself, but what He sees the Father do; for whatever He does, the Son also does in like manner" (John 5:19). We are called to do the same.

Our authority in Jesus Christ is based on far more than just attempting to "look big." Those who indeed live in His authority will grow to walk in confidence of their position as sons and daughters of God who have been seated with Jesus in heavenly places. When Jesus said that He would give us the keys of the Kingdom of heaven, it was based in more than a set of words. The authority of the believer in prayer exists because Jesus Christ released it to His Church by the price of His blood on the cross—a sacrifice that not only paid for our redemption, but also vanquished the devil (see Colossians 2:13–15). By this act He led captivity captive (see Ephesians 4:8) and has loosed the ties of sin's bondage for all who will come to Him.

TRUE LIBERTY

Second, let us understand liberty.

When we speak of loosing, we are talking about more than being set at liberty. We are talking about the reason for our freedom—the redemption that has been accomplished through the blood of the Lord Jesus Christ. We are also addressing a way of life. "Being freed" and "living free" are two different things.

Being freed is a moment . . . and certainly an important one. It pictures a prison cell having been unlocked and the chains loosed. But *living free* is a life pattern. It is depicted by our standing up, walking out of that prison cell and making daily choices to walk the path of liberty and live in the freedom bought for us at the cross. Galatians 5:1 says, "Stand fast therefore in the liberty by which Christ has made us free, and do not be entangled again with a yoke of bondage."

Being loosed is a call to a life in Christ, a call away from the things that indulge the flesh or "give place to the devil" (Ephesians 4:27). It is a call to live in the same way as the book of Hebrews describes the Bible's heroes of faith. They had an opportunity to return to the land from which they had come, but they sought a better place—what we would describe today as the "land of promise" or, to use another expression, the Kingdom of God.

We are always being called to new levels of freedom in Jesus Christ, and people who function effectively in spiritual life are people who learn how to let go and enter into every situation with Jesus' authority and Holy Spirit power.

CLARIFYING THE TERM *LOOSING*

Third, let us specifically define *to loose* or *loosing*.

Having made clear that the means of exercising prayer that "looses" requires authority, and that the objective is liberty, let's turn to the language of the New Testament to specify with clarity what Jesus intended to be understood when He said that whatever you loose on earth shall be loosed in heaven.

The Greek text uses the verb *luo*, and means "to unbind, to unfasten, to untie." One commentator describes this word as being able to "set free or deprive of authority." The text and its truth remind us of how many allow ourselves to be tied up—that is, taken captive, preoccupied to a point of distraction, disabled to live in liberty or living in condemnation and a lost sense of authority in Christ.

The nature of the bondage varies in individuals and, at times, involves believers as well as unbelievers. The Lord Jesus calls us, however, to minister to the captives, to loose them from invisible bonds and introduce the freedom He can bring at any point of human life or experience. The Word tells us that it was "for this purpose the Son of God was manifested, that He might destroy [*luo*] the works of the devil" (1 John 3:8). Because of the freedom promised us through the cross, the Adversary is now deprived of any authority to continue to bind, cage, captivate or sustain a hold on the person Jesus Christ frees.

Let's look at some examples of how the Lord Jesus worked new levels of freedom in the lives of people who discovered how to receive His loosing as it was ministered to bring breakthrough—to penetrate whatever the darkness oppressively had imposed. These were set free, loosed by the keys of the Kingdom through prayer and direct ministry.

LOOSED FROM SIN'S HOLD

A young couple once asked to meet with me for prayer prior to their entering a particular ministry role. I knew that these two were devoted to the Lord, but when I started to pray with them I sensed that something was amiss in their relationship with each other.

So I paused in praying and almost immediately the Lord gave me insight as to what we were dealing with. I asked the young woman to step out of my office for a minute so that I could talk with her husband. When she had left, I turned to him and said, "I don't want to embarrass you, but I'm going to ask you a very blunt question." I paused, engaging him eye to eye, not with a critical gaze but helping him feel my compassion and concern. I asked, "Have you either been unfaithful to your wife or had intercourse with her before you were married?"

Understandably he looked a little embarrassed, but he was clearly being truthful as he indicated he had never been unfaithful, but that they did have intercourse a number of times before they were married. I assured him that I was not condemning him but wanted to teach him something. I explained that when we fail to obey God's laws, we become entangled at the spiritual and psychological dimensions of our lives.

Sexual misconduct is just one of innumerable socially and culturally accepted behaviors that are rampant in our world today. Not only do non-believers embrace the world's system of indulgence, but Christians can muddle things just as badly. The challenge is that there are consequences when we compromise concerning the ways of the Lord. Even though we are seeking to serve Him, sin begins to weave a web around our feet. At some point we start to realize that something is not quite right. We have engaged in activity outside of God's order and, as a result, disorder has taken over. This couple, for instance, was not on the verge of splitting up, but they had concerns about their relationship. They were coping reasonably well, but God has not called us to be people who cope. He has called us to be people who conquer, and their victory required Kingdom keys of understanding, repentance and liberation.

I took a few minutes to explain the nature of "bonds" that entangle whenever God's ways are violated. The guilt of disobedience is not all that sin brings: Exposure to entangling strands of bondage also occur. God's warnings against sinning or disobedience are for far greater reasons than simply faulting us. His vastly greater desire is to guard us against the bondage it brings—bondage resultant because place has been given to the Adversary's kingdom. Those bonds are often released at the same time we come to Christ as Savior—that glorious moment that *all* sin *is* forgiven! Still, the residue of bonds put in place through willful disobedience may often linger until addressed with specific repentance—usually prompted by the Holy Spirit.

These occasions would well be likened to Lazarus' resurrection (see John 11:38–44). When Jesus called him from the grave, Lazarus "came forth" –instantly and completely *alive*. Jesus then instructs, "Loose the grave clothes and let him go." This very action magnificently describes the "post-new life" nature of some instances of freedom ministry when people have, as the young couple, willfully and as believers, indulged the flesh and disobeyed God's law. Now the Lord, in mercy and grace, was ready to free them unto their own ministry of freeing others.

I invited the young woman back into my office and told her what her husband and I had talked about, and then we began to pray once more. This time, however, we focused on loosing the unholy tie that was constricting them, holding them back. I prayed that through the power of the blood of Jesus Christ the unholy bond that had been established by disobedience—whether it was through ignorance or rebellion—be broken in the name of Jesus Christ.

The most beautiful thing started to happen. We could feel the liberty of the Spirit of God coming right then. The Lord did not want them launched out in the ministry that He had for them with the rubble of disorder at the foundation of their relationship.

At the heart of most "freedom ministry," the loosing of people from the snares of past disobedience needs to include teaching. Prayer against the darkness is effective because it introduces the Light—the truth of God's Word applied by the power of the Holy Spirit. So, with this case just described, let's review the basic keys that brought loosing into this situation.

- First, God's laws are for freedom.

They are not simply a list of religious prohibitions or divinely ordained restrictions for the sake of simply testing the will to obey. Take, for example, the issue of sexual purity: Presumably every thoughtful person would know that sexual fulfillment was designed by God, and the possibility of a fulfilling sexual relationship is intentioned within marriage. Not only did He invent sex, but He wrote the handbook for its most fulfilling expression and experience. The Creator knows how all life works best. And for this reason, all His laws are righteousness and peace, and are intended to be used that life be lived more abundantly rather than tied down or bound up through violating the very laws fundamental to our place in the created order of His benevolent design.

- Second, restoration from the bondage that disobedience to God's laws produces requires repentance.

Repentance is more than simply saying, "I repent"—the very word *repent* in the Scriptures involves a stance of the mind, a reversal of attitude, a turning from one direction to another. It is a choice. And it is a choice that can be made only in the light of God's truth, along with the understanding that is patiently and graciously offered to people who need to repent and find the freedom Christ offers.

These two facts will on occasion puzzle some who will ask, "Are you saying that, even though I've received Christ as Savior, become forgiven and been made a new creature in Christ, bondage may be present as residue from my past experiences? *Even though I've been forgiven?*"

The answer is not simplistic. To say yes can be misunderstood as saying that salvation is incomplete—as though receiving Christ and being born again does not ready you for heaven. Of course that is not true. Our salvation brings instant and complete "justification" through faith in Jesus Christ—the glorious reality that we have not only been forgiven, but that in the court where God alone judges humankind, He has declared us "not guilty." This position in Christ is conferred upon us by reason of our confessing ("receiving") Christ Jesus as the substitute sacrificed for our sin, atoning for ("covering" or "completely absolving us from") the record of sin in the courtroom of heaven.

However, as "ready for heaven" as we may be, completely received and regarded as "saints" in God's eyes, this is only the beginning point of our answering the call to grow in grace and in the knowledge of our Lord Jesus Christ. The Bible says we are now called to holiness, and that sanctification (or "growth into wholeness in all of life") is the will of God. Peter described this as answering the Father's call to "glory and virtue":

> Grace and peace be multiplied to you in the knowledge of
> God and of Jesus our Lord, as His divine power has given
> to us all things that pertain to life and godliness, through
> the knowledge of Him who called us by glory and virtue, by
> which have been given to us exceedingly great and precious
> promises, that through these you may be partakers of the
> divine nature, having escaped the corruption that is in the
> world through lust.
>
> 2 PETER 1:2–4

To continue in 2 Peter, as well as to study the teaching of the epistles and to clearly hear Jesus' charge to "take up [one's] cross daily, and follow [Him]" (Luke 9:23), is to discover that the presence of the Holy Spirit now dwelling in you will uncover or assist to discover points where freedom ministry needs to take place in each of our lives. It is in this regard that freedom ministry often deals with what I have often referred to as residual "fishhooks" and "fiery darts." The fishhooks represent the fact that we broke free of Satan's line that was drawing us to eternal death, but though the Liar's line was severed, something of the hook still awaits removal. The fiery darts are things that even the most sincere believer may encounter in spiritual warfare (see Ephesians 6:10–18).

Occasionally something lodges in the mind or emotions—some degree of success in an attack of the Adversary, yet which was not spiritually lethal. These things can become lodged and result in a spiritual infection that requires the sword of the Spirit—which divides between soul and spirit (that is, discerns between our spirit, which has been justified in Christ, and our soul, which still carries something of residue from the past, or the aftermath of an earlier assault).

Understanding these truths—the concepts of justification as well as sanctification—is essential. The first, justification, secures us with a sense of the profound fact of God's saving grace, which qualifies us for eternal life and the joy of being His sons and daughters *now*! The second, sanctification, reminds us that we are called to growth and that that pathway will introduce discovery or confrontation with things that still require loosing.

Scripture says, however, that because of what Jesus has done on the cross, a greater word has been spoken than any residual bond that binds a believer. A greater thing has taken place in the heavenlies—that is, in God's presence and before His throne—than anything that would bind us on earth. The application of Christ's victory to any temporal point of ongoing stumbling or entrapment can be immediately remedied.

Ministry into that situation with Holy Spirit–energized and empowered prayer, bringing to bear the glory power of the Lord, will "break every yoke" (Isaiah 58:6). Through the power of the cross of Jesus, whatever we loose on earth shall be loosed, dissolved, undone. Amen. And hallelujah!

SOWING AND REAPING

In another counseling session one time, a young woman with a solid foundation in the Word expressed a deep concern in her life. Her concern reveals another way that loosing works. "There is something that bothers me," she began. "Even though everything is together in my life now and I'm following the Lord, a verse in the Bible troubles me. Galatians 6:7–8 says, 'Do not be deceived, God is not mocked; for whatever a man sows, that he will also reap. For he who sows to his flesh will of the flesh reap corruption, but he who sows to the Spirit will of the Spirit reap everlasting life.' "

She went on to voice her concern that she was fearful of having children because in her own youth she had been rebellious and wild. "If I have children," she asked, "will I reap what I sowed? Won't I see in them the same seeds I planted?"

Her concern was understandable. This verse points us to a spiritual law: the law of reciprocity. Simply put, as we read above, we are going to reap what we sow. We see this concept other places in Scripture as well. Jesus says, for example, "Give, and it will be given to you . . . for with the same measure that you use, it will be measured back to you" (Luke 6:38). It is the same concept.

This concept had now raised a concern for this young woman. Even though she had repented of the seeds sown in her wild youth, still she feared that she would get more of the same. I had never had anyone ask me that question, and the Lord dropped a word of wisdom in my mind.

"Listen," I began. "When a person goes out and sows in a field, and there comes the harvest, then for there to be another harvest there has to be another sowing."

In other words, I explained, once you have had the harvest of "bad seed," then that harvest has taken place. No one needs to live a lifetime fearing that the cycle will continue time after time after time. The Lord has not condemned us to a lifetime of harvesting over and over again what we sowed only once. I knew that God was giving a simple but important principle: Once a harvest from unrighteous seeds has taken place, the tie is loosed.

I said to this young woman, "You've been sowing to the Spirit for the last several years, as far as I know."

She answered, "That's right."

"Then, according to what I read in the Scriptures, you don't have any harvest of corruption coming. That's been done. Now you have a harvest of eternal value coming."

She received those words with tears in her eyes, and fear and confusion were loosed from her heart.

If you have succumbed to the flesh, then repent. When you do, you will experience loosing from it. You might have to endure the consequences of your actions, but you will not reap over and over the effects of the sins. Each thing comes in its season. Once you have gone through a season of harvest, then take care how you sow after that.

TIME TO LET IT GO!

To conclude this chapter I want to discuss the most common point at which people succumb to bondage in their lives—unforgiveness. Unforgiveness is a Hydra-headed monster. Hydra was a multi-headed serpent or monster in Greek mythology, slain by Hercules. Each head, when cut off, was replaced by two others unless the wound was cauterized. Similarly (but unfortunately, it is no myth; it is hard reality), unforgiveness will manifest in multiple ways—bitterness, resentment, anger, vindictiveness, scornfulness, passive unresponsiveness, stubbornness, self-righteousness, even a steely silence or feigned, pretentious, "Oh, no, everything's okay with me," which is a façade for the fact that a low grade or deeply entrenched attitude is poisoning the soul and souring relationships.

I realize that is a very long sentence—not to mention a pivotally significant paragraph. Perhaps it deserves rereading—maybe a thoughtful review: "Lord Jesus, look into my heart." As David said, "Search me, O God, and know my heart: try me, and know my thoughts: and see if there be any wicked way in me, and lead me in the way everlasting" (Psalm 39:23–24, KJV).

Entire volumes are written on the subject of this sinister point of entrapment that not only restricts relationships, ruins households, splits churches, stresses neighborhoods and distances otherwise "decent" people from one another, but does more. Physicians say that a very high percentage of human affliction has its roots in unforgiveness and resentment. In short, our human frame, as created by our loving Father, is not equipped to withstand the poisoning power—in spirit, soul *or* body—of unforgiveness.

I want to relate a somewhat humorous story, although, having just completely addressed a heavy subject, it is not to lend a light touch. But I present it nonetheless because I think it illustrates the folly of our hearts, the ludicrous ways that unforgiveness can find access to our souls. I do not want to appear to trivialize the very real pain and anguish that have enveloped many people through abuse, brutality, hatefulness and plain neglect. These things wound deeply and often cause unforgiveness that only the Holy Spirit can heal as we accept His summons to let Him loose us from those bonds. But I want to conclude with an incident that may seem small at its occurrence but which became large in its outcome. The fountainhead of forgiveness must constantly flow forgiveness through us. The Holy Spirit prompts to "loose" at the start, something that could otherwise "tie us up," and disables our ability to live in freedom. So here's a "Sunday afternoon story" that may teach us together—an example of how "all tied" we can become, starting with a trivial thing that we can swell to ridiculous proportions—unless we "let it go." As I said, it was a Sunday afternoon years ago; I boarded a plane in Los Angeles to fly to Portland to speak Sunday evening.

It had already been a long day. I spoke in four services at The Church On The Way that morning and was now headed up north. Because of the strenuousness of the day, the host church for the Portland meeting had arranged first class travel so I could rest and get a little sleep before the evening time I would be ministering. Flying in "first" class also allowed quick exit of the plan, to assist on-time arrival at the church, since a small closet for those in that part of the airplane was provided.

As I boarded, I handed my light-weight garment bag to the flight attendant so that she could hang it up, and as I did, she looked a little embarrassed. "Sir," she said apologetically, "I don't think there's room for it here."

I looked around, and saw that there were just a few people in the first class cabin, counting me, and knew there should have been plenty of room. I did not doubt her, but I leaned over my seat and looked in to see about ten garment bags crammed in there, and the closet was jammed!

Now, I know well how tedious it is to use the closet in the back of the plane provided for those flying coach or economy. It seems to take forever to wait for everyone else to get off the plane so you can go back there and get your bag. I did, in fact, need the convenience. However, I reasoned to myself, either everybody in the first class cabin has three garment bags, or the negligent attendants let people in the coach section hang their things in the closet supposedly "Reserved for First Class."

You can sense how this is stacking up as a very petty issue. I said nothing to the flight attendant; didn't express irritation (at least openly!), but was aggravated inside, because this airline's service isn't taking care of its job! And the one "suffering" for it was . . . well, me! (Sounds of violin music in the background, themed to my "pain.")

Somebody has to set this right, I thought. So I sat down, said nothing, but my mind was working overtime. I was "ticked," as we say, and I thought, I'm going to write the airline's customer relations! Now, mind you, I was gracious to the flight attendant. (After all, "I'm a Christian!") But inside a thing called self-righteous selfishness was gradually taking over; being a fog cover for how readily our own "being right" (actually, self-righteousness) can be a convenient term to use for one's own unforgiveness, criticism, judgmentalism, irritation.

So, there I was, irritated and building up a head of the steam of my own self-righteousness. In my letter to customer service, I decided, I would give all the facts. I was pretty sure the rear closet was not full because there were not that many people on board, but I thought I had better check. So I stepped into the aisle.

As I did, I heard a still, small voice quietly communicate, Sit down and let it go!

The principle of loosing was being pressed into my heart by the Holy Spirit—and I knew it.

It's embarrassing to face yourself at times—even more so to face your Lord when you know He's correcting you, and ignoring Him is not really possible if you're honest-to-God "for real." But there I was, Mr. Global-Corrector-of-All-Injustice starting toward the back to "righteously" check the closet in the back of the plane, irritated with the airlines and with the flight attendant, and tired from the morning. Now, I also thought it "fair" of me to check the rack in back and see if it was full—thus excusing the attendant in my cabin for yielding my closet space to others. (Isn't this story disgusting!)

Little did I know that about four seats from the back a four-year-old boy was drawing with a wide-tip, black marker. Nor did I know that at the very moment I was passing by he would want to show his mother the picture he had drawn. Nor had I anticipated how, if you are four years old, if one hand holding artwork should go toward the seat your mother is in, the other hand should swing out the other way, and as the felt-tip marker swung out over the aisle, I saw it coming but could not avoid contact. And in one smooth streak, my light gray slacks had a black stripe displayed prominently . . . and I had none to change into as I headed for the service.

The echo of the words Sit down and let it go had twice rebounded in my mind as I had walked up the aisle, but now I weighed the irony of the moment. I was getting ready to fire off a letter to the airline, but God took the hand of a four-year-old boy and wrote me one first. And I know what it said: SIT DOWN AND LET IT GO!

I knew it. And I knew then, I would not write the letter, but . . .

But I was so close to the back. My mission now "for information only" needed only about five more steps. So I took them, and just as I was within reach of the closet, one of the plane's spring-loaded containers holding soft drinks popped open. . . . Soda cans rolled everywhere, and I nearly fell down when one hit my foot!

Well, the fact is—I was right—there were almost no garment bags back there, and no justification for the attendant "giving away my space"! But it was a hollow victory, because neither was there any justification for my sudden granting of a "small souled attitude" to "bind" me—even for the two minutes that whole episode involved. I returned to my seat, got buckled in, looked down at the ink stain on my slacks and said, "Lord, forgive me for my foolishness . . . for disobeying Your speaking to me; and I thank You for patient persistence in correcting anything in me so self-serving or unforgiving."

Let me tell you something: We can tie ourselves in knots without anyone even knowing about it. If I had stayed in that frame of mind, I would probably have dissipated 95 percent of the spiritual energy that I needed to be released in ministry that evening. (The fact is, that evening there was a great spiritual breakthrough in that congregation—one for which I had been graciously "loosed" to minister—but I am convinced that I would not have been equipped for it if I had remained "bound" by even so small a thing as my personal convenience.

There are so many ways, things, circumstances we can tie ourselves up with, but the Spirit of God calls us: Loose it, and let it go.

Dear one, we do not have to control everything. As we let go, whatever we loose on earth is released in the spiritual realm so that we are not shackled for effective operation.

As I already noted, the story I have told can seem trivial, but unforgiveness begins—oh too often—with "little things," and unforgiveness is so rooted in our human nature. We so easily yield to unforgiveness, to criticism, anger or resentment—and they all "bind." But Jesus said that if we forgive (that is, "loose"), you will be forgiven (Luke 6:37). Jesus also knew that we would need to "practice" forgiveness. That should be an encouragement to us! If it can be "practiced," it can be learned, improved, and become a habit of our lives. Matthew 18:21–22 records how open-heartedly we should forgive:

Then Peter came to Him and said, "Lord, how often shall my brother sin against me, and I forgive him? Up to seven times?" Jesus said to him, "I do not say to you, up to seven times, but up to seventy times seven."

Jesus was not encouraging Peter to keep a scorecard of how many times he forgave each individual; rather, he was encouraging Peter to "go against the grain" of what is so easy for humankind.

Each time we forgive, we also effectively let go of our right to judge. Hebrews 12:23 says that "God is the judge of all"— judgment belongs to Him and Him alone. Letting go of judgment, and learning to forgive, is another way that we see His will done "on earth as it is in heaven." People who function effectively in spiritual life and power are people who learn how to "let self and selfishness go."

We may talk all we want about dominion over demons, or seeking to command them to come out in Jesus' name. We can try to right every wrong and heal every wound. But if we are bound or tied up in a self-imposed straightjacket of unforgiveness, we will compromise the "grace flow" of the Spirit which alone can "loose" Kingdom powers. Jesus came to set us free—He came to loose us, so that we can be open countenanced, large-hearted liberators—freed and freeing to effectively penetrate the darkness of the world around us.

Living in the liberty which Christ has given us, prayer with power, ministry with authority, joy in faith and love toward all will make us effective Kingdom warriors—ready to engage the battle for lost souls and broken people.

9

ENGAGING IN BATTLE

For the weapons of our warfare are not carnal
but mighty in God for pulling down strongholds.

2 CORINTHIANS 10:4

I really enjoy watching movies about our nation's history, both documentaries and historical fiction. One time I was watching *The Patriot* and was struck by one particular scene. In case you have never seen this movie, it is set in the time period of the Revolutionary War. The main character is a widower with seven children. Having fought in a previous conflict, he knows the horrors of war, and now his main goal is to keep his family out of the war. Thus he plays it safe and refuses to take a stand; he is now pledged to peace at any cost. His older sons are anxious to fight, anxious to engage the enemy, anxious to take the stand their father refuses to take. But though they argue and pressure him, he remains firm in his resolve: "I will not engage the enemy for the safety of my family."

But the enemy comes and finds him.

This man tries at one point to be humanitarian to some

injured Colonial soldiers. Just then he turns around to see the Redcoats marching through his fields to his home. Enraged at his kindness to their enemy, the British soldiers shoot all the Colonial wounded, take the man's oldest son captive and set fire to his home. In an instant, his life has changed, and he has no choice but to enter the battle.

Sometimes we do the same thing when it comes to our Adversary, the devil. We act as though if we play fair, the devil will leave us alone. But we need to come to grips with the fact that the devil is not just some little character that sits on our shoulders telling us to steal the cookie out of the cookie jar. He is vicious, relentless and completely committed to the destruction of humankind. Like the man in the movie, we can go about our lives and refuse to take a stand, but the point will arrive when the battle comes to us.

In this chapter we will look at effective fervent prayer that engages the battle against the kingdom of darkness with the power of the Kingdom of God. This kind of prayer calls for earnestness and fervency in prayer that moves into the invisible realm where evil has dominated a situation, and then breaks the yoke of bondage over those circumstances. This is prayer that confronts the work of hell and casts down the rule of darkness that is hindering God's intended blessing for that situation.

I want to say to you pointedly that every believer needs to face the responsibility of letting his life be enlarged by this dimension of prayer. If you want to see release or breakthrough happen in your life and in the lives of those you pray for, then there are times when you will need to enter the battle in a fervent pursuit of prayer—breaking in on the works of darkness and seeing them shattered by the power of the word of God that comes forth from your lips. There is no substitute for that kind of confrontational prayer.

Throughout the New Testament, the apostle Paul uses the metaphor of battle. Indeed, Jesus alluded to it when He talked about taking the Kingdom by force (see Matthew 11:12). So the concept of warring against the works of darkness is not some sensationalistic idea that someone came up with to whip people into a frenzy of prayer. Nor is it something to stir us against people. Scripture pointedly teaches that "though we walk in the flesh, we do not war according to the flesh" (2 Corinthians 10:3). We are not fighting against people.

So what are we doing? First, we are fighting "the good warfare" (1 Timothy 1:18). Though Jesus is the Prince of Peace, peace always comes at a price. We are called to wage a battle that is "good"—the battle that establishes God's rule on earth as it is in heaven. Second, we are waging that war against the powers of darkness (see Ephesians 6:12). We have already studied the fact that this has to do with the invisible, spiritual realm. But we have to be convinced not only that that realm exists, but that we have been commissioned to do battle there. We often look at prayer warriors as people who are particularly called or anointed to ministry in this way. Yet God calls all His children to this kind of prayer.

WHO CAN PRAY THIS PRAYER?

The Bible says that "the effectual fervent prayer of a righteous man availeth much" (James 5:16, KJV). The Message version words it this way: "The prayer of a person living right with God is something powerful to be reckoned with."

"Well," you might say, "if that's the criterion, it automatically excludes me! It says that 'righteous' people are empowered for this kind of prayer. It says that 'right living' makes us powerful in the Spirit." Again, it has to do with recognizing that God has called and authorized all His children to pray this kind of prayer. According to Scripture, the righteous person is anyone who has been forgiven and made right with God through the blood of Jesus Christ and is following in the way of the Lord.

When we reject the fact that we, too, are called righteous (see Romans 5:17–19), we hamstring ourselves and our effectiveness by choosing to live in a convoluted arrogance that is actually saying that "my sins are the only ones Jesus couldn't fully forgive." Nor is a righteous person someone who has acquired a self-developed sense of holiness. Our own righteousness is nothing more than filthy rags (see Isaiah 64:6). But when we are clothed in the glory of the Lord, it is as though we have traded in our own garments and received the garments of righteousness (see Isaiah 61:10) through Jesus Christ. Then we can come before Him boldly and with a sense of confidence (see Hebrews 4:16). He has called us to live like fully forgiven, fully accepted, fully empowered sons and daughters of the Most High God. Once we accept His gift of righteousness, we can pray the "effectual fervent prayer" that James talks about.

As we begin our study on fervent prayer, it is best for us to look at two initial points that James introduces. The first is that he describes this kind of prayer as "effectual fervent" prayer. The Greek word used here is *energeo*. The literal definition is "to be active or efficient"; but you can see the obvious connection to our English word *energy*. This is prayer that is energetic! In fact, for the concept even to be communicated in English, the translators used two words to translate *energeo*— "effectual fervent."

It may also help our understanding to look at the English definition of those two words. *Fervent* is defined as "exhibiting or marked by great intensity or feeling," and *effectual* as "producing or able to produce a desired effect." The kind of prayer James is writing about here has great intensity and great passion—but it produces the desired effect!

The second point James introduces is an Old Testament example of this New Testament truth. James tells us that Elijah was a man of "like passions as we are" (KJV) and yet he prayed that it would not rain, and it did not rain for the space of three and a half years (see James 5:17). Then he prayed that it would rain, and it did. Here is a man praying fervently—praying with the energy the Holy Spirit gives. This is prayer that transforms circumstances and releases the blessing of God into a time and place where it has not been moving.

By the way, it is important for us to see biblical episodes like the one we are about to observe not only as an academic approach to Scripture, but also as evidence of the total integration of the Old and New Testaments. In 1 Corinthians the apostle Paul instructs that the Old Testament accounts "were written for our admonition, upon whom the ends of the ages have come" (1 Corinthians 10:11). These are not just Sunday school stories or religious myths; these are accounts of people who lived life as we do. And we are supposed to learn from their testimonies. So James turns us toward Elijah, describing him as "a man subject to like passions as we are." This is a man like us; in other words, every one of us, according to James, has access to this same kind of influence through prophetic prayer. Just like Elijah.

A WORLD OF EVIL

The story of Elijah is told in 1 Kings, and the episode we are going to look at is found in chapter 18. The first verse gives us a basic outline of what fervent prayer is all about, and the later parts of the chapter show us the principles that apply.

This account begins telling us that "it came to pass after many days that the word of the LORD came to Elijah, in the third year, saying, 'Go, present yourself to Ahab, and I will send rain on the earth' " (verse 1). There are three important concepts present in this one verse: the concept that sin and drought are connected; that God uses ordinary people just like us; and that the Word of God confronts evil. Let's look at how these concepts are lived out.

Evil Invites Drought

No rain had fallen for three years. This is exactly what Elijah had prophesied (see 1 Kings 17:1). He had reminded Israel's King Ahab of a principle God had proclaimed to Moses long before. God had said, "If the people do not obey My commands, I will change your rain to powder and dust" (see Deuteronomy 28:15, 24). Elijah had wanted Ahab to understand at the outset that the coming drought was a direct action of God and a direct result of Israel's sin. The Lord would be functioning through the instrument of weather.

I am convinced, by the way, when something like that happens, it is not so much a case of God's depriving people of blessing as it is God's releasing them to their own desires. When people continually choose sin, God releases them to what Satan will give them. It is as if He is saying, "Go ahead. If drought is what you want, you will see what that dark kingdom functions like, because Satan was a thief, a robber, a murderer from the beginning" (see John 8:44).

Satan is the god of drought. He lives in a dry place. We know this because Jesus said that whenever demonic spirits pass out of a man they go into "dry places" (Matthew 12:43). Remember, we are talking about the spiritual, invisible realm. I am not saying that the devil lives in the Sahara Desert or any other physical dry place. We are talking about the fact that in the spiritual dimension, the Adversary's hometown territories are devoid of the flow of the river of God's Spirit. Thus, when people surrender to works of darkness, they welcome that kind of problem. And because we live in the physical realm, those spiritual choices will eventually be seen there as well. Consequently, in 1 Kings, we see that the rule of King Ahab was a manifestly evil rule that defied God's blessing and invited drought.

Ahab was king of Israel and the husband of Jezebel, who was the daughter of a pagan king. Jezebel brought the worship of Baal with her, and Ahab joined her in enthroning her Canaanite god and its companion god, Asherah. The worship of these gods was sinister, merciless, manifest evil. It was what we would call in our time Satanism and involved the sacrifice of human life. The word *Baal* means "master." It was grinding mastery of the personality, working toward its destruction. It was a religion of fear, perversion and death.

The worship of Asherah was a horribly indulgent, perverted expression of what today anthropologically is called a fertility cult, meaning the worship of and indulgence in perverted sex in exchange for the god's granting abundant crops. What God has ordained to be pure and powerful and fulfilling in human experience was perverted and diluted and debased in every form.

The products of those licentious unions were children who were presented to the god and consumed. As a matter of fact, archaeologists have unearthed altars to these gods, which have included thousands of jars containing the bones of infants and young children. I think much could be said as we look at our own culture and its deteriorating attitude toward the life of infants.

It does not strain the text at all to say that Ahab's reign is a picture of any instance in which evil moves in to dominate. Ahab was an evil king; Satan is the king of evil. In any circumstance where we see the rejection of God's intended blessing, we see drought in some form. In this instance, in an agricultural society, the loss of the continuous certainty of rain was more than a passing inconvenience.

This principle suggests an important parallel for our own experiences. The dry spell described in 1 Kings was a result of a manifestly evil rule. Every single one of us either has experienced or is experiencing or will experience a time when we can see nothing growing. It is a dry spell. Those dry spells can show up in many different ways and different circumstances. There can be a downturn in your business. You may see something wonderful beginning to take place in your life, and it suddenly . . . dries up. There are periods when, time after time, you see something getting cut off before it can come to fruition. These are dry spells. Droughts. No less real than a physical drought of rain. These seasons occur because the rule of the invisible powers, thrones, mights, principalities—the work of darkness—has moved in to dominate that situation and thereby reject the blessing God intended for it. When we face these kinds of situations, where drought is ruling, we can step in just as surely as Elijah did.

Ordinary People and Powerful Prayer

The description of Elijah is one of a man who was subject to life's passions as we are. He was not immune to depression, despair or despondency. I am sometimes convinced that Elijah was the kind of guy who woke up irritable some mornings. In fact, we could easily draw the conclusion that he woke up irritable every morning! Elijah even describes himself to the Lord as "very zealous" (1 Kings 19:10). The Hebrew word used there literally means "to envy, be jealous, be envious, be zealous." Elijah was passionate about God, blunt in how he addressed people and, well, kind of quirky. We see a lot of these same attributes in John the Baptist who, Scripture tells us, came in the spirit of Elijah. Bottom line—these guys did not give you the warm fuzzies.

When James refers to this prophet, he makes clear that Elijah's prayer of faith was not based upon superhuman transcendence of the flesh and its weaknesses. He did not walk around radiating imaginary holiness, robed in white and making wise and powerful utterances. He was a man subject to the same feelings and emotions that we experience. And it is this same "ordinary guy" who Scripture says prayed and no rain fell for three and a half years. When he prayed again, rain fell.

This is who James chooses to illustrate how effectual fervent prayer works. The New Testament application of this dramatic Old Testament story should come as no surprise to any of us. Living on this side of the cross, we sometimes forget we are living in the continuum of God's workings. God has always been God; He has always been at work. As surely as Abraham looked ahead and rejoiced to see Jesus' day (see John 8:56), we can look back and access the promise of God's past workings. The Bible tells us that "Jesus is the same yesterday, today, and forever" (Hebrews 13:8). Every lesson and work of God that we see in His timeline of redemptive history can be applied to our own lives. The life of Elijah is just one example of the miracle workings of God that can be claimed by any of His children. It is Elijah's story; it is James' story; and it is designed to become my story, and your story, too.

The Word Confronts Evil

First Kings 17:1 gives further insight. At the beginning of this drought Elijah had said to Ahab, "As the LORD God of Israel lives, before whom I stand, there shall not be dew nor rain these years, except at my word." Here was a man who understood, before Jesus ever explained it, that whatever we bind on earth has been bound in heaven, and whatever we loose on earth has been loosed in heaven. Elijah was saying, "God told me, and I'm telling you. This is what He has determined in heaven, and when it comes down to earth, it will be exactly as He has said."

This is not arrogance. There is a world of difference between praying with expectancy and praying with presumption. Praying with fervency and expectancy requires that we live as people becoming more and more familiar with the voice of the Lord, so that we know how to pray. Expectancy hears the voice of the Lord and then moves into prayer to see His will done on earth. In contrast to praying expectantly, presumption or presumptuous prayer tells God what we think ought to happen and demands that He act. In the case of Elijah, the Spirit of God was causing a man to understand God's desire for righteousness to be made manifest for the redeemed. When God's people stand before the Lord and sense His heartbeat, when they realize that He desires for His people to come out from under the bondage of hell, then they will declare and experience deliverance.

When the Lord was ready to end the drought, He told Elijah to go show himself to Ahab. He was sending His prophet to confront the one who was ruling in the realm of evil. The objective? To release blessing. God wanted rain upon those people and He wanted to give evidence of His blessing upon

His prophet. But that cannot happen without the confrontation with evil.

THE TRUE GOD SHOWS UP

Elijah, in obedience to the Lord, showed himself to the king. The situation is almost humorous in its predictably accusing response of the enemy. Here is a man who has heard the voice of the Lord and obeyed Him; and he is immediately challenged, accused and blamed by Ahab. As soon as King Ahab saw Elijah, he challenged, "Is that you, O troubler of Israel?" (1 Kings 17:18).

How often has that happened to any one of us? We are listening for the voice of the Lord, praying in obedience to Him, and the Adversary takes that moment to begin to accuse and remind us of everything wrong we have ever done. Let me hasten to remind you—we have no right to come before the throne of heaven and intercede for our world without the power of the cross of Jesus Christ. In essence, the Adversary is right: We are not worthy. But when we stand as penitent and forgiven sons and daughters of the living God, the Accuser has no right to us.

Elijah stood his ground: "I haven't troubled Israel. It's you and your father's house. It's all of you who have forsaken the commandments of the Lord and followed Baal. You've got the wrong guy. It's you. You're the man."

Elijah then proposed a test to prove who was the true God. Ahab readily agreed. With the 450 prophets of Baal and the additional 400 prophets of Asherah in attendance, they would cut up a bull and lay the pieces on an altar up on Mount Carmel. After they had offered their sacrifice and called on their god, then Elijah would offer his sacrifice of a second bull and call on his God.

The God who answered by fire from heaven and consumed the sacrifice would be recognized as the true God.

Beginning in the morning, all the prophets of Baal went through their contortions and their rituals and their incantations to try to make some miracle power happen. Scripture says that Elijah actually started to mock them. He was bold because he knew their god was not going to be able to deliver. He said, "Call a little louder—he is a god, after all. Maybe he's off meditating somewhere or other, or maybe he's gotten involved in a project, or maybe he's on vacation. You don't suppose he's overslept, do you, and needs to be awakened?"

From morning till evening the prophets called on the name of Baal, cutting themselves with knives and lances until blood gushed from their bodies. Let me just point out that when Scripture says "there is nothing new under the sun" (Ecclesiastes 1:9), it is really true. When we look at young people cutting themselves in self-destructive behavior, make no mistake that the demon beings behind the idol Baal are still at work in our world. They may present themselves differently, but when the result is the same, it is the same principality behind the action.

The prophets of Baal did their best, but there was no response from heaven. Toward the end of the day, Elijah stepped forward, and Scripture says it was "at the time of the offering of the evening sacrifice" (1 Kings 18:29). They are perhaps some of my favorite words in Scripture. After the frenzied antics of Baal's prophets, there is a breath of simplicity and peace in those words. Elijah stepped up and said, "Now it's my turn."

In order to give evidence that there was no chicanery or fraud, he commanded that water be poured three times into a trough around the sacrifice he was offering. Then in a prayer of some sixty words, he called on God for an outpouring of His power.

The Bible tells us,

> Then the fire of the LORD fell and consumed the burnt
> sacrifice, and the wood and the stones and the dust, and it
> licked up the water that was in the trench. Now when all the
> people saw it, they fell on their faces; and they said, "The
> LORD, He is God! The LORD, He is God!"
>
> 1 KINGS 18:38

It was a proven point of victory, but there is more to learn from
Elijah. This victory did not come about without certain things taking place. And in this passage we can also see four ways the prophet
modeled for us to confront darkness with fervent prayer.

Rebuild the Broken Altar

Once the prophets of Baal were finished, Elijah began "his
turn" by calling the people to him and directing them to repair
the altar of the Lord that had been broken down. If you seek
breakthrough when confronting evil, then begin by rebuilding
the places where there are broken altars.

While broken altars can be in a nation (as this one was), or
within a church or a family—really within any group of people—
the first place to look for a broken altar is in your own life. I
want to make clear that it is not my goal to place upon you—or
me—a burden of condemnation. My purpose is to help us see
that certain developments must take place in our lives if we
intend to confront evil that is hindering the will and purpose of
God. These can be any area that we have let slide—disciplines
or obedience that the Lord has called us to. One important one,
if we will learn to enter into confrontational, fervent prayer and
see the workings of evil broken down, is to begin by building
an altar of prayer.

Jesus made the commitment to build a Church that the gates of hell could not prevail against, and we see here evidence of that principle in operation. Anything of a passive stance in prayer, anything that takes a casual attitude, will not achieve the depth, passion or inner conviction that spiritual warfare requires, and that the Lord desires for us to pursue.

Now we do experience times in prayer that are very simple, times that are refreshing, times that call for rejoicing. But here we are talking about the times where fervency—the energized, impassioned prayer—of a redeemed and made-righteous person avails much. The Lord is calling His people to ever-deepening dimensions of prayer in which we are on our faces before Him and seeking hard after Him. This is where the groaning pours from within (see Romans 8:26). This is not something mystical but is, rather, a place where you feel deeply that the workings of the darkness have hindered what God wants to do, and you come against those dark powers in the name of the Lord. Triumph in all spiritual conflict begins with a person who will build an altar to confront evil with prayer.

Call on the Name of the Lord

The second way Elijah modeled for us to confront darkness is to recognize that our only ground of authority is the name of the Lord. First Kings 18:32 says that Elijah "built an altar in the name of the Lord." The New Testament tells us that it is only in the name of Jesus that we can be saved (see Acts 4:12), only in His name that we have been given authority over principalities and powers (see Mark 9:38–39; Acts 16:18), only at Jesus' name that every knee will bow—that is, acknowledge and yield to His will (see Philippians 2:10).

Not one of us could be saved except for the sacrifice accomplished by Jesus. We come to God through His Son, the Lamb that was slain for us. By the same token, no spiritual victory is ever accomplished without drawing on the resource of that sacrifice.

I think it would be good for us to understand the intensity of the conflict by seeing the bleeding and battered body of Jesus on the cross, and then listen to Him in His resurrection as He announces to His disciples, "All power is given to Me in heaven and earth. You go and extend My Kingdom" (see Matthew 28:18). That directive is accomplished as believers move in the power of prayer.

Elijah's actions thus foreshadowed the power of the cross where the blood of Jesus Christ flowed to break the yoke of bondage. Through the cross Jesus made an open show of the works of hell. As surely as Elijah came to offer the evening sacrifice in the name of the Lord, we come in Jesus' name—"who for the joy that was set before Him endured the cross" (Hebrews 12:2). What was that joy? That as a result of His sacrifice, He could bring us to salvation and empower His Church to apply the triumph of His sacrifice to the situations we face.

Deal with the Enemy

The Bible says that at Elijah's prayer, the fire fell and consumed the sacrifice, the wood, the stones, even the water in the trough. But that was not the end of it. Elijah immediately directed the people to take the prophets of Baal down to the Brook Kishon, where he slew them.

If this seems a bit intolerant or narrow-minded, we need to remember that God's dealings with Israel are uniquely within the covenant He made with them, a covenant to which they agreed. The majority of His judgments in the Old Testament need to be understood in that context. Deuteronomy 27 and 28 relate the reading of the covenant to Israel as they are getting ready to go into the Promised Land, and clearly state the blessings on obedience and curses on disobedience before all the people. The understanding was foundational that there were consequences for not walking in the way of the Lord as the new nation was about to step into her inheritance. Further, the Lord clearly stated earlier in the Law of Moses that leading people astray through idolatrous worship was grounds for capital punishment (see Deuteronomy 13:6–10). Now Elijah, with the help of the penitent people, executed that judgment.

Please understand, the application for us is not the decision to fight evil by going around burning up pornography studios or bombing abortion clinics. Ours is not to believe that the Church will ever be assigned the task of exacting judgment on evil. God reserves that task entirely as His own. Our battle, again, remember, is *not*—nor ever will be—against flesh and blood. We are talking about confrontation in the spiritual arena. We do not wrestle against flesh and blood, but against spiritual hosts of wickedness in the heavenly places.

The third way, then, that Elijah modeled for us to confront darkness was to pursue the enemy to complete overthrow. Once we begin to see God answer, don't stop there. We are to go on and pursue the enemy until he is brought completely underfoot. "The God of peace will crush Satan under your feet shortly" (Romans 16:20). Let me challenge you: How often do you begin to see the breaking of the enemy's hold over a situation in your family, your workplace or your town, and you become so excited about what has begun that you stop praying? Yes! We should thank the Lord for the beginning signs of victory, but that does not mean we should stop pursuing the battle. We accomplish such pursuit by continuing to set aside time two or three times a week to say, "Lord, I continue to press in regarding that battle until the enemy is trodden underfoot, as You said. Jesus promised in Luke 10:19 that we will trample on serpents and scorpions, not just chase them. We will pursue them to the ground."

If what happened to Elijah had happened at some prayer meetings when the blessings, the power or "the fire" falls, that would have been the end of the prayer meeting right there. Everybody would have become caught up in the excitement of manifestations that are simply the beginning. But the goal is not the beginning of a victory; it is in seeing the victory become established. This is what the Bible means when it speaks of triumph. "Now thanks be to God who always leads us in triumph in Christ" (2 Corinthians 2:14). The Lord has called us beyond simply experiencing a demonstration of His power. He wants to achieve a total release of His blessing, and calls us—as godly people years ago would often say—to "pray through."

Call Forth Blessing

Finally, Elijah knew that dealing with the enemy was not the final step. If you have ever studied any of the rebuilding that had to take place in Europe after either of the twentieth century's world wars, you will understand when I say that the end of battle can leave a pretty barren landscape. This is what Elijah faced. There had been no rain for more than three years. He knew that facing down the enemy cleared the stage for God to begin His redemptive action within the culture. Now it was time for rain.

The fourth step outlined here is this: After the previous three things have taken place, we still must seek God until the final breakthrough comes. This is not a time of confronting the Adversary. It is a time to prayerfully seek to see God's order of things reinstated.

After the confrontation between Elijah and the prophets of Baal, Elijah said to King Ahab, "Go up, eat and drink; for there is the sound of abundance of rain" (1 Kings 18:41). At this point in the story there was not even a cloud in the sky. Where did Elijah hear thunder? Where did he hear wind and oncoming rain? He heard it in the Spirit; he saw it in the invisible realm. His prayers were not out of desperation, hoping that everything would work out. Rather, Scripture tells us that he cast himself on the ground and put his face between his knees. That was nothing other than the squatting position taken in that culture for a woman laboring to give birth. Elijah was entering into travail.

Elijah prayed for a while, then said to his servant, "Go up now and look toward the sea. Look out toward the Mediterranean and tell me what you can see." We are not told how long the servant had to walk. I doubt it was just a few steps to the brow of a hill. It is my guess he had to trudge upward for some minutes to get a view of the sea.

His servant came back and said, "There's nothing."

Elijah said, "Go. Go again." He said this seven times: "Go. Go again."

Finally, the seventh time Elijah's servant trudged back to his vantage point of the horizon, he saw a cloud. He reported that there was "a cloud, as small as a man's hand, rising out of the sea!" (verse 44). It was just one cloud, and he could block the view of it with his fist.

Elijah said, "That's enough. God is in action." The blessing of rain was evident and Elijah's task was completed. The next verse tells us that "it happened . . . that the sky became black with clouds and wind, and there was a heavy rain" (verse 45).

The effective fervent prayer of one person like you, like me—like us—effected the entry of God's hand of power unto the working of miracles.

This brings back our understanding of Matthew 11:12 as we saw in our first chapter. Jesus said that "from the days of John the Baptist until now the kingdom of heaven suffers violence, and

the violent take it by force." If we are going to see the birthing of
Kingdom life into present circumstances, I believe the Bride of
Christ, the living Church, needs to enter into participation.

Confrontation with evil is not a matter of trying to stir God
up so that He will act; it is a matter of people who have become
so deeply stirred by the destructive works of hell around them
that they pray with fervor until they see the blessing of God
break in.

FERVENCY EQUALS ENERGY

Elijah had said that no rain would fall except at his word.
Three and a half years later, God told Elijah that the time had
come: "I give you My word. It's going to rain now." Yet still we
find Elijah imploring God time and time and time again. Elijah's
actions do not make sense to us if we look at prophecy as the
quick-fix answer and do not take action. Prophecy is given for a
purpose: It tells us what is released in the heavens; prayer releases
it on earth.

This is no small thing! And it is the reason we need to grow
in our faith and boldness in prayer. God has determined that the
Spirit shall be poured out upon all flesh before the return of the
Lord Jesus. That is the prophetic word on the subject, and with
it God is calling us to employ forceful, sustained praying to see
His will done "on earth as it is in heaven."

The point is not that our energy or zeal compels God to act.
We are not manipulating God; we are being invited to partner
with Him with the same passion He has. When we deal with
great issues that occupy our passions and we begin to seek the
Lord fervently in the dry spells, then we confront the powers of
darkness. As we do that, we will begin to see evil broken and the
rain of God's blessing fall (see Deuteronomy 28:12).

That is what is given to us by promise in Scripture. It is what James meant by telling us that the effective, energized prayer of a person made righteous in Jesus counts for a lot. I have been impressed by the bold translation of this verse Dr. Richard C. H. Lenski provides in his commentary on the epistle of James. One might be inclined to think this renowned and respected Lutheran scholar would have hesitated noting the following possibility that would suggest too great a role of prayer as the means to bring about God's workings. He says, "A righteous one's petition avails a great deal when putting forth its energy. In other words, the release of righteousness is related to the energy with which the petition is delivered."

Now you might say: Run that one by me again. The power of God is released in proportion to the energy with which my petition is delivered? The answer is yes. There is clearly a connection between the passion in prayer extended from our earth side of things, and the release of God's operational power from the heaven side. This relatedness of the passion of prayer is also seen in biblical cases when fasting is united to prayer. So let's be well advised: There is no reason to feel that bold, passionate or urgent prayer should be trivialized on the grounds that emotion is either unimportant or inappropriate. There is a biblical connection between prayerful, humble yet bold faith and the breaking of the powers of hell.

I want no one to conclude that by your works or my works we can manipulate God into doing anything. Never, *never* think that! But neither allow yourself to think that bland, halfhearted prayers are going to accomplish much. An absence of passion is no sign of maturity. Believers who seek the introduction of God's works of power into those circumstances where an overthrow of the Adversary or an entry of God's miracle grace is needed must be bold in prayer. James writes that what accomplishes much is *effectual fervent praying.* We are talking about a man, a woman, even a child whose heart is learning to beat with that same heart of passion God has to see His Kingdom come and will be done "on earth as it is in heaven."

This is the kind of prayer that confronts the works of darkness—anything from hordes of fallen angels and demonic workings that need to be disentangled to the mass of failure of millions upon millions of people lost in sin. God is calling for people who, like Elijah, will come before Him in a spirit of travail, setting themselves to pray . . . again and again and again and again. You and I must seek God until the answer comes. We don't stop. That is the kind of prayer that can turn any situation around.

10
INVASION OF LIFE

I labor in birth again until Christ is formed in you.

GALATIANS 4:19

Let me tell you the story of a woman I am going to call Jeannie, and her daughter, Ashley. I had known Jeannie for years, had been her pastor for decades. She was as stable and settled a woman in her walk with the Lord as there ever has been. She was not given to the "mystical," but was a solid, head-on-straight, common sense, spiritually discerning person.

But she was having a hard time with her daughter. With Ashley.

Ashley was a good girl. She loved the Lord and was involved in our youth group. She was a godly spiritual influence in her high school. And yet . . . there had been an ongoing spiritual battle regarding this girl that had gone on for years, and it was over the issue of yieldedness. Ashley had not learned to ask for help or submit herself to guidance. She "always had a better idea."

Typical teenager, you might think. But Jeannie was taking

this extremely seriously. After all, yieldedness is at the heart of how we are called to respond to the Lord.

But *this* day . . . Jeannie had reached her limit.

She was sitting at her desk that morning completely discouraged and unutterably weary. She was ready to give up. She had gotten two kids through this stage, and was coming to the conclusion that maybe Ashley was going to have to learn that particular lesson as an adult, perhaps experiencing the price of her own self-will and headstrong stubbornness, in frustrated relationships, unnecessary contentions and wasted possibilities of her own future.

With that day's sense of "ineffectiveness in a seemingly unending battle," Jeannie put her head down on her desk at home, and prayed. *Lord, I'm just so tired of dealing with this issue. And I want to stop now.*

Later, she described how immediately she began to feel (in her words) "the Holy Spirit get big in me." Jeannie went on: "I felt a supernatural strength begin to flood me. It started at my feet and began to spread upward with such strength that I *had* to stand up! And as I stood, I knew that by my action I was confronting the Adversary who would cause me to give up before the battle was over.

"I knew there were words to be spoken, too," she continued. "So as I stood, I verbally confronted that spirit of discouragement: 'I will not lose this one! Two out of three odds is not good enough when it comes to my children!' Commitment to seeing the battle through to the end was galvanized in me with that action and with those words, through the empowering of the Holy Spirit."

In the following weeks, the Lord pressed this burden of prayer and confrontation into Jeannie's heart as never before. Sometimes she would pray in the Spirit; other times she would simply groan in prayer before the Lord—something she had never experienced. And the Lord gave her a Scripture: "I travail in birth again until Christ be formed in you" (Galatians 4:19, KJV). Paul is writing here about the anguish and concern he felt in prayer for the Galatian church to realize their potential and promise in Christ Jesus. The only comparison Paul could make was to that of a woman in labor.

This is travailing prayer.

Travail is, of course, a word often used in referring to labor or birth pains. In the original text, it is the word *odeeno,* and forms of this word occur seven times in the New Testament, always in reference to instances where something of the "birthing" of God's redemptive workings is entering our world! So, when we talk about travailing prayer we are talking about prayer that labors until something of the Kingdom is born in a situation. We have already seen one illustration of travailing in prayer as we looked at the life of Elijah in the last chapter. As we explore this type of prayer more closely, let's look first at the way Jesus used that word.

THE BEGINNING OF SORROWS

In Matthew 24, as Jesus was prophesying about the end times, He spoke of the "beginning of sorrows" (verse 8). He foretold a number of events that will occur before His return. Some of these events have occurred throughout history, but the intensity of their occurrence in our world today—such as an increase and intensity of frequency of earthquakes, war and disease—suggests that we are living exactly in the time Jesus spoke of as the "beginning of sorrows."

I am not entering into this discussion for prophetic timeline purposes, however. My goal here is to explore the term *beginning of sorrows* for descriptive purposes. The word used here for *sorrows* is the word for *travail.* This is the word that describes the pains and agonies of birth. Here Jesus uses that laboring word to point to the particular transition period in history when His Kingdom will be fully birthed into this world.

The apostle Paul used a related word when he described how the "whole creation groans and labors with birth pangs together until now" (Romans 8:22). What the earth is yearning and travailing for is the day in which the Lord Jesus Christ returns as King, along with the hosts that will be with Him at His appearing—not only angels, but also sons and daughters of God. When that takes place, Paul said, it will fulfill the "yearning" of creation. So in the teaching of both Jesus and Paul we find this expression of the throes of agony preceding the rulership of Jesus Christ on this earth.

Now we are part of God's creation, of course, and if by our travailing and longing for His return we could shorten the time before His appearing, I suppose that we could get quite excited about the possibilities. But I am not describing the prayer of travail because I think we can change the return date of Jesus. There does not seem to me to be any scriptural evidence to indicate that we can "hasten His coming," even though at times we will hear this phrase used. The Bible does urge our obedience and passionate pursuit of global evangelism and ministry in every way we can touch the world, so my observation is not to suggest passivity or a casual attitude in any way. But, let us remember that the Bible says no one knows the day or the hour in which Christ shall come again; only the Father knows. Jesus Himself said that it had not even been disclosed to Him (see Matthew 24:36).

So though we cannot, through travailing prayer, affect the time of Jesus' coming, we do have reason to believe in the possibility of a "new world" being born in people's hearts and lives—*now*—in families, in businesses and, yes, even in the flow of history being written around us. God's will and working—the entry of the Kingdom—may be birthed into the midst of *any* human situation—not in the sense of His millennial rule but in the sense of His present, redemptive activity.

The Kingdom of God can penetrate the darkness of any human circumstance now, *today*, when it is invited in. This means that whenever we face hopelessness, we still cling to hope. Whenever we face destruction, we accept the possibility of reconstruction. Whenever we face mourning, we expect God to bring forth joy. That is the "stuff" of which Paul wrote when the Holy Spirit breathed upon him as he wrote to the Corinthians,

> But we have this treasure in earthen vessels, that the excellence of the power may be of God and not of us. We are hard-pressed on every side, yet not crushed; we are perplexed, but not in despair; persecuted, but not forsaken; struck down, but not destroyed.
>
> 2 CORINTHIANS 4:7–9

Likewise, when the prophet Jeremiah penned the oft-quoted words that God will give us "a future and a hope" (Jeremiah 29:11), he was writing to a nation captive in Babylon.

In the days of His earthly ministry, Jesus told His disciples that the Kingdom of God was within them and to go spread that message abroad. He was declaring that, in His name, there was no situation of darkness or despair that could not be transformed by the life-begetting power of His Kingdom and His authority. He who is the way, the truth and the life expected then, and expects today, this transforming power to flow through His Body.

THE NEED FOR TRAVAILING PRAYER

It is imperative to understand this concept of travailing as we watch the last days—"the beginning of sorrows"—as they unwrap around us. There is a helpful added insight regarding travailing prayer in Isaiah 26:16–18:

LORD, in trouble they have visited You, they poured out a prayer when Your chastening was upon them. As a woman with child is in pain and cries out in her pangs, when she draws near the time of her delivery, so have we been in Your sight, O LORD. We have been with child, we have been in pain; we have, as it were, brought forth wind; we have not accomplished any deliverance in the earth, nor have the inhabitants of the world fallen.

Isaiah uses the verbal picture of a woman in birth pains to describe the ineffectiveness of God's people to effect change in the world around them through prayer. It is often no different for us. In applying the prophet's words to the Body of Christ, it says that "we have been with child"—in other words, "the Kingdom of God is within you," and me.

Further, "we have been in pain"—this is the weight we feel over certain circumstances. But are we finding effectiveness in prayer? If the answer is no, then we have, as Isaiah said, "brought forth only wind." We have not been successful in accomplishing "any deliverance in the earth, nor have the inhabitants of the world fallen." This text is saying that there are times of trouble when we neither work deliverance for God's people, nor work destruction against the evil around us.

God's Word calls us to come against the works of darkness. This is what He came to do. "For this purpose the Son of God was manifested, that He might destroy the works of the devil" (1 John 3:8); and He expects us to continue that kind of overthrow against the enemy. He wants to enable us, in the spiritual realm, to break down the invisible, but real, strongholds of hellish conspiracy. Yet, the prophet notes a people who "have not worked any deliverance," describing those who do not know their privileged access to God's power; nor are they walking in the authority He has given.

How often do sincere believers pray because it is "the right thing to do"? Yet perfunctory prayer can become little more than "idle chatter" (Proverbs 14:23), without inquiry of the Holy Spirit about how He would direct or enable their prayer. In travailing prayer, we cannot afford to "just pray." We are called to focused, travailing prayer that intentionally seeks the will of the Father— that understands what He has called us to accomplish, and then earnestly prays effectually, fervently—seeking God to see Kingdom life birthed into the world around us.

BEAR DOWN

The simplest way that I know to describe travailing in prayer is with the words I have heard nurses say to my wife when she was giving birth. When the labor pains began to intensify, and the moment of birth drew near, the nurse would say to her, "Bear down, honey. Bear down. Bear down."

I believe that God wants to teach us how to see the works of darkness destroyed, but it will happen when serious "bearing down" in prayer is directed by the Holy Spirit and responded to by believers in Jesus Christ. How do we know when such an appointment is ours? Well, perhaps you have begun to bring a matter before the Lord in prayer, but you feel a deepening concern. As that concern rises within you, take time to "bear down," perhaps only for a few minutes, but pray until you receive a sense of release, just as it is when a contraction passes with a mother's labor. At times, as with labor pains, that rising urge to pray will come again, and possibly repeat many times periodically over a number of days or weeks. The Lord will put the burden—the contraction—on you again for travailing prayer until that situation is birthed unto new life. Like a mother's labor at birthing, there is not a set time for travailing prayer, which may be for a few hours or in another case for days. But when the believer opens to the Holy Spirit's prayer partnership, presses in and begins to pray with intensity, His leading will prompt the frequency, until the effectual fervent prayer has been fully offered and the birthing of divinely enabled and begotten answers will be revealed.

Such prayer is not a matter of gender, but of faith and commitment to birth the Kingdom power of Jesus Christ into circumstances, into families, into impossible situations. When exercised, the glory of His rulership, victory and purposes will break forth with *life*—life brought forth by travail.

STRENGTH TO GIVE BIRTH

We want to have effectiveness in prayer, but travail also requires strength. One of my daughters once said that "laboring in birth" was aptly named . . . it was the hardest work she had ever done! The prophet Isaiah addresses this aspect of travail as well, thus introducing us to another point of understanding what labor, or travail, is.

In Isaiah 37:3, we read that "the children have come to birth, but there is no strength to bring them forth." At this time, Jerusalem was under siege, and the nation was facing death-dealing adversity. The Assyrian army was ensconced against Jerusalem, and its general was making bold threats. At this point in history, Assyria was the world's dominant power. Judah's king, Hezekiah, knew there was no way that Jerusalem could stand up against this army. The Jewish nation had diminished in size and strength by more than 80 percent, both in their military force and their territory. Now, the overwhelming nature of the situation was such that Hezekiah and all the people were crippled by fear, feeling like a mother whose child had come to the birth, but no strength remained to enter labor—they were weak, spent and helpless.

It was then that the prophet Isaiah sent Hezekiah a prophetic word, and summoned the king to call on the Lord. The prophet's earlier mention of "no strength to bring forth" would not determine the outcome. Strength for victory would not be based on human energy, but on the will to pray—to *ask anyway*! The message speaks to us all when we face situations feeling as though we have reached our limit. In such moments our strength is to call on the Lord; the strength to bring forth victory is His—ours is to pray no matter how weak we feel. Frankly, it is not "bad" to feel you are in a hopeless place—never! Though from our side of things it looks as though all hope is gone, it forces us to a dependence on the Lord we may not have come to otherwise.

The apostle Paul writes of a similar moment in his life, a time he had prayed multiple times with no answer forthcoming. It was in the face of his weakness that the Lord answered him, "My grace is sufficient for you, for My strength is made perfect in weakness" (2 Corinthians 12:9).

There is even more for us in the Word to speak to occasions when we come to the end of our strength. Romans 8:19–27 describes times we virtually ache with longing for the full and final redemption of God's purposes in our world. But, praise God! There is a Holy Spirit-provided sufficiency for such moments—again, one described as travailing prayer that realizes a breakthrough of life, hope and deliverance. In that context God's Word says "the Spirit also helps in our weaknesses . . . [and] makes intercession for us with groanings which cannot be uttered . . . according to the will of God." The message is clear: When we find ourselves at our weakest, the Holy Spirit is available to come alongside us with *His* strength to enable us to pray beyond what *our* strength allows. We have all faced situations when, like David, we cry out, "My strength fails me" (Psalm 38:10). But, again, thank the Lord, we never are limited to reliance on ourselves. He who gives strength to the weak and strengthens us by His Spirit will give us adequacy in prayer. For we can do all things through Christ Jesus who strengthens us (see Philippians 4:13). Not only does He give us strength to pray with fervency, but He gives us strength to travail, to birth life and light into the darkness.

THE TRAVAIL OF JESUS ON THE CROSS

We would be remiss if we did not also look at the concept of travail in the life of Jesus. God wants to see the life of His Son, Jesus, in us—to see the image of His Son brought forth in us. In other words, He is ready to grow in us the grace that will work in us the same traits we see in Jesus, including something of the nature of His willingness to travail—to let Him teach us to pray in that way.

We earlier noted the reference in Isaiah 53:12 to Jesus' interceding on our behalf. This same passage includes the concept of travail. As the prophet describes in graphic detail the suffering Messiah, he writes:

> He was taken from prison and from judgment, and who will declare His generation? For He was cut off from the land of the living; for the transgressions of My people He was stricken. And they made His grave with the wicked— but with the rich at His death, because He had done no violence, nor was any deceit in His mouth. Yet it pleased the LORD to bruise Him; He has put Him to grief. When You make His soul an offering for sin, He shall see His seed, He shall prolong His days, and the pleasure of the LORD shall prosper in His hand. He shall see the labor of His soul, and be satisfied. By His knowledge My righteous Servant shall justify many, for He shall bear their iniquities.
>
> ISAIAH 53:8–11

Note the prophet's statement "He shall see His seed," while a few verses before he says, "Who will declare His generation? For He was cut off from the land of the living." These words do not merely affirm that Messiah would sire no biological children, but the text proceeds to make clear there would be a birthing through His travail: "He shall see the labor [travail] of His soul, and shall be satisfied." Clearly, the travail Jesus had to do was for the securing of redemption by which He would bring sons and daughters to the Father—born spiritually unto eternal life. The combination of Jesus' intercession in Gethsemane—crying out in prayer, sweating drops of blood—joined to His suffering and death on the cross describe that travail. If there is ever a picture of "bearing down," this certainly portrays it dynamically. The outcome, as described in the Word, was that He brought many sons to glory (see Hebrews 2:10) and "as many as received Him, to them He gave the right to become children of God" (John 1:12).

The Father says, "All those who come out from among the nations and come to Me, I will be a Father to them and they will be My sons and daughters. They were birthed into life through My Son" (see 2 Corinthians 6:17–18). Thus, through the travail of His soul, Jesus continued to see His seed and rejoices in the fruit of His "labor." Even on Calvary He "[endured] the cross, despising the shame" being sustained "for the joy that was set before Him" (Hebrews 12:2). As a woman forgets the pain of labor for the joy over the child that is born (see John 16:21), so it was with Jesus. For the joy that was set before Him, anticipating the day He would see you and me brought forth into life—our deliverance, our health, our joy, our fulfillment—for that joy He saw the cross as something He was willing to bear. And now He sees the travail of His soul and is satisfied.

FROM CONCEPTION TO DELIVERY

The Bible gives another beautiful picture of the way the Lord's purposes work in us in the person of Mary, who conceived seed from the living God and brought forth His Son. We, too, are to receive God's promises, conceive in faith, carry in hope and deliver by the power of the Holy Spirit.

Now, none of us is going to experience a virgin birth . . . that's been done! But Mary does offer us a pattern of openness to hear God, immediate response and humble obedience that is unparalleled.

The references to Mary in the New Testament are relatively few, yet what is revealed is a picture of a person who simply says yes to God. Perhaps the most moving of references to Mary is in Acts 1:14. She is in the Upper Room, seeking God with the disciples as, together, they wait for power from on high. If anyone in the world had a reason to flaunt spiritual achievement, it was Mary. "Don't tell *me* about hearing from God. . . . I've seen angels, I've experienced things no one else will ever experience. *And* I raised the Son of God." She had every human right not to press in, every reason to say her purpose had been fulfilled. But she humbly comes with the rest of the disciples to seek God for the next thing He wants to do. Perhaps it was this attribute of Mary that opened the door for her to bear the Christ child in the first place.

Our first encounter with Mary is, of course, when the angel comes to her to announce that she will be the mother of the Messiah. Again, while none of us will receive that promise, there are promises that the Lord wants to release in and through each one of us. As with Mary, God is looking for people who, with childlike faith, will receive the promise and say yes to Him.

Mary's promise was, as we know, a literal conception. Yet how often have we believed and received a promise from the Father, then not allow it to take root and grow in us? God is calling us, through the Holy Spirit to—in faith—conceive the truth of His Word. "Lord, I believe Your promise is true. I believe You want to work this. I believe You want to see this done. I believe that Your power will overrule the darkness. I believe the Kingdom will enter this situation."

Then you begin to carry that promise, and to carry it for the necessary season. How long do we carry things in prayer? For as long as the Lord calls us to. Sometimes we need just to speak once and then let it rest. Other times the Holy Spirit will say, *You bear that along.* When He does, our response is not to mope along. A healthy woman carrying her child often experiences her greatest radiance. I think a person who is really under the touch of Jesus carrying a thing in prayer will not have an attitude of drudgery. This is not a time of defeatism, negativity or skepticism: "I don't know if it's going to work out." Rather, at these times we should have special radiance and confidence as we stand on the promises of God's Word.

Then comes the time of delivery. It might not be hard to receive in anticipation, to conceive in faith and to carry in hope, but when it comes time to deliver we find out how sincere we really are about seeing new life birthed in *this* situation. In exasperation, or frustration, or weariness in waiting, we are tempted to stop praying for a person . . . a circumstance . . . a family . . . a promise. Change never comes, however, without travailing prayer. When the first generation of believers in our family began to pray, it took forty years of travailing prayer to see every relative come to salvation in Christ. Travailing prayer *cannot* give up halfway through labor—every "contraction" is met in prayer unto the birthing of new life.

Whatever circumstance you have been called to travail for, this is the time to bear down in prayer, to stand in strength by the power of the Holy Spirit, so that new life issues forth. The Lord is looking for those who will join in the fellowship of His sufferings, travailing to see the powers of darkness pushed back in the world around us. Only He can make possible this kind of prayer.

11
WE SHALL DO VALIANTLY

Through God we will do valiantly,
for it is He who shall tread down our enemies.

PSALM 108:13

We have seen in the pages of this book that prayer is a work we are invited to, and the invitation is to every believer. It is a call to partnership with the One who has given His life for us. It is a call to extend His Kingdom, seeing His life and light penetrate the darkness of evil that surrounds so many.

How are you going to answer that invitation?

When it comes to invitations, many of us immediately come up with our stock excuse list, which I have found mostly centers around time—not having enough of it or, in the case of a "prayer invitation," thinking that the limited amount you do have is not enough to make a difference.

First, let me assure you: God is eternal. Time is not an issue for Him. He simply invites us to partnership and obedience. We talked in the last chapter about the fact that some "labors" are short and some are long. The fact is, He is inviting us to pray.

Second, many of us fear what we do is not enough. And let me say here: You are right. It will never be enough; because neither the invitation nor the response is based in works. They are both based in grace. In Ephesians 2:8–10, the Bible tells us,

> For by grace you have been saved through faith, and that not of yourselves; it is the gift of God, not of works, lest anyone should boast. For we are His workmanship, created in Christ Jesus for good works, which God prepared beforehand that we should walk in them.

Everything has been provided for us by grace; everything has been won for us on the cross of Jesus Christ—our salvation, and the good works God invites us to walk in.

So it may never "be enough," but it also "counts." My daughter Rebecca has worked on this book with me, and she told me a story about her husband, Scott. Scott was a pastor for almost thirty years, and passionate about prayer. But when he was a young college student at the University of California, Los Angeles, he had his eye on medical school. In one of his science classes, he had to do an experiment with two beakers of clear liquids that, when combined, would turn pink.

This was a tedious experiment and involved adding one of the liquids to the other one drop at a time to determine *exactly* how many drops it took for the liquids to change color. He described the agonizingly slow, and seemingly mundane, task of counting drops and seeing no change. Minutes passed, drops went in, marks went on the tally sheet. Then a drop of liquid went in that changed color for a split second but then went clear. There were several more of those, when finally—the decisive drop—*and in an instant everything changed.*

He told this story once in a class that he taught on prayer.

When he finished telling the story, he looked at the class and asked two questions:

Which drop was more important in seeing change effected?

And, when you pray . . . which prayer is more important?

Of course, there is no answer to "Which drop is more important?" because he needed every one of those drops to see the change take place.

I believe it is much the same with prayer. I do not know how prayer is "measured." I am sure it is not measured by vain repetition, or shouting, or figuring out formulas. But there is evidence in Scripture that many things are measured by the Lord. Consider this:

- When we are facing sorrow, the Bible tells us that God keeps our tears in a bottle (see Psalm 56:8). That is infinitely tender to me; the Lord knows what sorrow has cost you and me.

- The wicked King Belshazzar was told that God had weighed him in the balances, and he had been found wanting (see Daniel 5:27).

- In the book of Proverbs, the word *ponder* is from a Hebrew word that means "to weigh." Proverbs 20:10 says that "Diverse weights and diverse measures, they are both alike, an abomination to the Lord." Why? Because God ponders, measures and judges fairly.

- Sowing and reaping has something to do with measuring. Matthew 7:2 says, "For with what judgment you judge, you will be judged; and with the measure you use, it will be measured back to you."

So which prayer matters more?

They all matter. When we accept the invitation to pray, we begin sowing the seed of seeing God's Kingdom extended into the earth, into people's lives. We begin to see the darkness of "this present evil age" (Galatians 1:4) pressed back and overthrown. Paul writes, "Let us not grow weary while doing good, for in due season we shall reap if we do not lose heart" (Galatians 6:9).

And that is where patience comes in. Prayer is real; but it is easy to discard when we do not get the answer we want as fast as we want.

Consider these words of Scripture:

- Paul wrote that "we must through many tribulations enter the kingdom of God" (Acts 14:22).

- John wrote that he was our "brother and companion in the tribulation and kingdom and patience of Jesus Christ" (Revelation 1:9), and later, "You have persevered and have patience, and have labored for My name's sake and have not become weary" (Revelation 2:3).

- James taught: "My brethren, count it all joy when you fall into various trials, knowing that the testing of your faith produces patience. But let patience have its perfect work, that you may be perfect and complete, lacking nothing" (James 1:2-4).

- Jude exhorted the brethren to "contend earnestly" (Jude 1:3).

There is a very real struggle that we are involved in. None of this is said to discourage, but to *encourage you* to keep contending! While not every "battle" may turn out as we want it, we can rest assured that the ultimate victory has already been won on the cross of Jesus Christ. Our part of the "partnership" is to— "continue earnestly in prayer, being vigilant in it with thanksgiving" (Colossians 4:2).

So . . . how are you going to answer the invitation?

We have been invited to "put on the armor of light" (Romans

13:12) and penetrate the darkness, overthrowing the dark powers that seek to engulf our world. We have been invited to intercede and see the lives of those we love changed in the name of Jesus. We have been invited into a partnership with the living, loving God of the universe—who through the cross has become our Father and now calls us to "walk as children of light" (Ephesians 5:8).

There is no more certain truth than this: The darkness cannot stand before the onslaught of light. From the inception of the "Word becoming flesh," with the entry of the Light of the world coming to introduce the Kingdom, this has been declared:

The light shines in the darkness, and the darkness has never been able to overcome it (see John 1:5)!

So, dear one, lift up your head, and your eyes as well—your head, because it is to His glory that our "heads" (i.e., our authority) have been lifted, intended to be raised in hope, in faith and with love by people who believe—truly believe—that God is wholly desiring to reveal His love, life, grace and power on earth as it is in heaven. And lift up your eyes—fixing your eyes on Him—especially in times such as ours that indicate our drawing very, very close to His appearing (see Luke 21:28; Hebrews 12:2). If we direct our vision, with faith that looks up with steadfast expectancy, not only will we be moving ever closer to the ultimate manifestation of His redemption, which is drawing near, but we will experience His "redemptive entry" into many situations that without penetrating prayer would not be realized.

So be encouraged by His Word and promise. Lay hold of what the Holy Spirit may have enlarged to your understanding, and your sense of confidence and faith in prayer.

Join hands with me, and with the hosts that are being awakened by the Spirit of God, to face this hour with understanding, boldness and a will to "warfare prayer"—always in the light of the cross, the "final conquest"—which takes those steps that will unleash the power of God's purposes and will here on earth as it is in heaven.

It is that order of believer that will penetrate the darkness—"that you may become blameless and harmless, children of God without fault in the midst of a crooked and perverse generation, among whom you shine as lights in the world" (Philippians 2:15).

With that charge, let's move together in this promise the Word has given, and I leave with you: *For with God we will do valiantly—it is He who shall tread down our enemy.*

A PRAYER FOR
RECEIVING CHRIST
AS LORD AND SAVIOR

It seems possible that some earnest inquirer may have read this book and somehow still never have received Jesus Christ as personal Savior. If that is true of you—that you have never personally welcomed the Lord Jesus into your heart to be your Savior and to lead you in the matters of your life—I would like to encourage you and help you to do that.

There is no need to delay, for an honest heart can approach the loving Father God at any time. So I would like to invite you to come with me, and let's pray to Him right now.

If it is possible there where you are, bow your head, or even kneel if you can. In either case, let me pray a simple prayer first and then I have added words for you to pray yourself.

MY PRAYER

Father God, I have the privilege of joining with this child of Yours who is reading this book right now. I want to thank You for the openness of heart being shown toward You and I want to praise You for Your promise, that when we call to You, You will answer.

I know that genuine sincerity is present in this heart, which is ready to speak this prayer, and so we come to You in the name and through the cross of Your Son, the Lord Jesus. Thank You for hearing.[1]

And now, speak your prayer.

YOUR PRAYER

Dear God, I am doing this because I believe in Your love for me, and I want to ask You to come to me as I come to You. Please help me now.

First, I thank You for sending Your Son, Jesus, to earth to live and to die for me on the cross. I thank You for the gift of forgiveness of sin that You offer me now, and I pray for that forgiveness.

Forgive me and cleanse my life in Your sight, through the blood of Jesus Christ. I am sorry for anything and everything I have ever done that is unworthy in Your sight. Please take away all guilt and shame, as I accept the fact that Jesus died to pay for all my sins and that through Him, I am now given forgiveness on this earth and eternal life in heaven.

I ask You, Lord Jesus, please come into my life now. Because You

---

[1]Jack Hayford, *I'll Hold You in Heaven* (Ventura, Calif.: Regal, 2003), 38–39. Used by permission.

rose from the dead, I know You are alive and I want You to live with me—now and forever.

I am turning my life over to You and from my way to Yours. I invite Your Holy Spirit to fill me and lead me forward in a life that will please the heavenly Father.

Thank You for hearing me. From this day forward, I commit myself to Jesus Christ, the Son of God. In His name, Amen.[2]

---

[2]Ibid., 39–40.

A PRAYER FOR INVITING THE LORD TO FILL YOU WITH THE HOLY SPIRIT

If you would like to invite the Lord to fill you with the Holy Spirit, here is a prayer you may wish to use. I am not asking you to say "Amen" at the end of this prayer, because after inviting Jesus to fill you, it is good to begin to praise Him in faith. Praise and worship Jesus, simply allowing the Holy Spirit to help you do so. He will manifest Himself in a Christ-glorifying way, and you can ask Him to enrich this moment by causing you to know the presence and power of the Lord Jesus. Don't hesitate to expect the same things in your experience as occurred to people in the Bible. The spirit of praise is an appropriate way to express that expectation; and to make Jesus your focus, worship as you praise. Glorify Him and leave the rest to the Holy Spirit.

Dear Lord Jesus, I thank You and praise You for Your great love and faithfulness to me. My heart is filled with joy whenever I think of the great gift of salvation You have so freely given to me. And I humbly glorify You, Lord Jesus, for You have forgiven me all my sins and brought me to the Father.

Now I come in obedience to Your call.

I want to receive the fullness of the Holy Spirit. I do not come because I am worthy myself, but because You have invited me to come. Because You have washed me from my sins, I thank You that You have made the vessel of my life a worthy one to be filled with the Holy Spirit of God.

I want to be overflowed with Your life, Your love and Your power, Lord Jesus. I want to show forth Your grace, Your words, Your goodness and Your gifts to everyone I can.

And so with simple, childlike faith, I ask You, Lord, to fill me with the Holy Spirit. I open all of myself to You to receive all of Yourself in me.

I love You, Lord, and I lift my voice in praise to You. I welcome Your might and Your miracles to be manifested in me for Your glory and unto Your praise. Amen.

Jack W. Hayford is Founding Pastor of The Church On The Way in Van Nuys, California, and Chancellor of The King's University in Los Angeles. He is also founder of the Jack W. Hayford School of Pastoral Nurture—a ministry that has impacted thousands of pastors from more than fifty denominations and numerous independent groups. In travels, he speaks to more than twenty thousand church leaders annually and has ministered in more than fifty nations. Jack has also written more than forty books and composed nearly six hundred hymns and choruses, including the internationally known "Majesty." His radio and television ministry has extended throughout the United States and into most parts of the world. He also serves on numerous boards of Christian ministries and agencies.

Jack and his wife, Anna (she, too, is a licensed minister), have been married for more than fifty years, having united while in their junior year of college. They entered public ministry beginning as youth ministers in 1956 and have served together in pastoral ministry as well as in fields of education. They are both graduates of LIFE Bible College in Los Angeles, and Jack also graduated from Azusa Pacific University. In 1998, APU designated him as the university's Alumnus of the Year.

Additional information may be obtained by contacting:

The King's University
14800 Sherman Way
Van Nuys, California 91405

or

www.kingsuniversity.edu
www.jackhayford.org

Rebecca Hayford Bauer has served in pastoral ministry for more than thirty years, and is a professor at The King's University, as well as at "Foursquare Ignite"—a discipleship school for students just out of high school. She has taught every age group, from babies to senior adults; served as a women's ministries director; published several books; and developed a parenting curriculum. She teaches on building the life God desires for you, marriage and family, discipleship and processing grief and loss. She works on writing projects, speaks widely and is a certified life coach. She received her education from LIFE Bible College (1979) and Regent University (2002). She is also the author of the award-winning book *The 25 Days of Christmas*.

Rebecca and her late husband, Scott, were married for 27 years. She has three grown children and eight grandchildren.

Additional information may be obtained by contacting: www.rebeccabauer.org